the *essential*
GUIDE TO
MANAGING
TALENT

To Mark, Louise, Charlotte and Annabelle Sinclair for your constant love and inspiration, and for always being there for me.

Kaye Thorne

With thanks and appreciation to my wife (Brenda) and family (Sarah, Kes and Jordan) for putting up with me locking myself in the basement and to Kaye for putting up with me – full stop!

Andy Pellant

With appreciation to numerous clients and customers who have trusted us to work with them on the key areas of talent and talent management.

the *essential*
GUIDE TO
MANAGING
TALENT

How top companies recruit, train & retain the best employees

Kaye Thorne & Andy Pellant

**KOGAN
PAGE**

London and Philadelphia

Publisher's note

Every possible effort has been made to ensure that the information contained in this book is accurate at the time of going to press, and the publishers and authors cannot accept responsibility for any errors or omissions, however caused. No responsibility for loss or damage occasioned to any person acting, or refraining from action, as a result of the material in this publication can be accepted by the editor, the publisher or any of the authors.

First published in Great Britain and the United States in 2007 by Kogan Page Limited

120 Pentonville Road
London N1 9JN
United Kingdom
www.kogan-page.co.uk

525 South 4th Street, #241
Philadelphia PA 19147
USA

© Kaye Thorne and Andy Pellant, 2007

ISBN–10 0 7494 4463 0
ISBN–13 978 0 7494 4463 1

British Library Cataloguing-in-Publication Data

A CIP record for this book is available from the British Library.

Library of Congress Cataloging-in-Publication Data

Thorne, Kaye.
   The essential guide to managing talent : how top companies recruit, train, and retain the best / Kaye Thorne and Andy Pellant.
        p. cm.
   Includes bibliographical references.
   ISBN 0-7494-4463-0
   1. Employees—Recruiting—Case studies.   2. Employees—Training of—Case studies.
   3. Employee motivation—Case studies.   4. Job satisfaction—Case studies.   5. Employee retention—Case studies.   I. Pellant, Andy.   II. Title.   III. Title: Managing Talent.   IV. Title: How top companies recruit, train, and retain the best.
HF5549.5.R44T467 2006
658.3—dc22

                                                                                    2006018808

Typeset by Datamatics Technologies Ltd, Chennai, India
Printed and bound in India by Replika Press Pvt Ltd

Contents

Acknowledgements

We would like in these acknowledgements to pay tribute to our families, friends, colleagues, clients and fellow authors to whom we owe a great debt of gratitude for their ongoing care, support and inspiration.

We would also like in particular to thank the following individuals and companies who willingly gave their time and support in taking part in our research and the case studies:

Alan Stanhope, Former Principal, Cornwall College
Alex Machray, previous co-author
Ali Gee, Wise Monkey, 3 Monkeys Communications
Angie Moxham, Chief Monkey, 3 Monkeys Communications
Ann Elliot, HR Director, Portman Building Society
Ann Moreira, Leadership Development Manager, Autodesk
Bronte Blomhoj, People Person, innocent drinks
Caitlin Hammond, Senior Learning and Development Manager
Catherine Salway, Group Brand Manager at Virgin Management Ltd,
Christine Bennett, Head of Talent Management and People Development, Department for Transport
Claire Brooks, Remuneration and Policy Manager, Portman Building Society
Clayton Glen, Commercial Director, HDA

David Mackey, previous co-author

David Parks, Vice President, Business Development, Bluepoint Leadership Development

David Rowlands, Permanent Secretary, Department for Transport

Debbie Carter, Editor, *Training Journal*

Deborah Moran, Independent Consultant, Epona Associates

Dennis Preston, Change Management Consultant and Executive Coach, anagram

Des Benjamin, CEO, HSA Group Limited

Ian Anderson, Former Community Investment Director, Whitebread

Ian Banyard, Independent Consultant, Epona Associates

John Kenney, Independent Consultant

Julian Duxfield, HR Director, Department for Transport

Kate Hennig, Senior Project Manager, Tenon Academy

Kevin McGrath, Business Development Manager, Assessment and Development Consultants

Klaus Duetoft, Director, Irrelach Consulting Pty Limited, Australia

Llorett Kemplen Independent Consultant, Communicashone

Mairin Gannon, Head of Management Training and Development, Universal Music

Malcolm Swatton, SVP of HR, Universal Music

Mark Day, Director PMI and HR, HSA Group Limited

Mark Woodhouse, previous co-author

Michael Pye, Director, HR Operations, Universal Music

Peter Honey, psychologist, author and management consultant

Peter Wheeldon, People Adviser, Virgin Management Ltd, part of The Virgin Group of Companies

Robert Sharpe, CEO, Portman Building Society.

Will Keith

All the authors mentioned in the references and recommended reading, all the staff at the CIPD and IOD libraries for their help in compiling the bibliography. Helen Kogan, Viki Williams and the rest of the team at Kogan Page.

Finally all our very special clients and the individual talented people who took part in our various talent and *Managing the Mavericks* surveys and who ultimately have been our inspiration. Our grateful thanks to you all.

Introduction

Talent, like innovation and creativity, is highly desired, yet rarely understood or effectively nurtured within organizations. Many recruitment advertisements ask for talented people, yet if organizations are lucky enough to recruit a talented individual they often experience difficulty in engaging or retaining them.

Faced with these challenges, what we have tried to do is to identify some of the issues around talent and to identify organizations that have acknowledged the challenges but that have sought to find positive ways of overcoming them. Within this book you will find organizational case studies, personal views about talent, and the results of research that we have undertaken over the years. As well as focusing on talent, we will also draw on some of the research undertaken for an earlier book, *Managing the Mavericks* (2003) by Kaye Thorne, which specifically looked at talented people who are pushing the boundaries of their talent. If you want to read more about how we undertook our research there are full details in Chapter 12: The basis of our research.

THE JOURNEY TOWARDS SUCCESSFUL TALENT DEVELOPMENT

Our approach has been as follows.

In Chapter 1 we seek to open the debate about talent, to identify some definitions and to highlight some of the challenges.

One very real issue is that talent development is often managed through disparate parts of HR policy or strategy. Rarely is there a coherent and coordinated approach that is shared throughout all functions and at all levels in the organization. In addition, HR still has a long way to go in being accepted as a key player in formulating business strategy and so entering into any meaningful and enduring debate about talent becomes a challenge. We explore how HR can enter into a strategic debate in Chapter 2: The strategic role for HR.

We suggest that talent cannot be considered in isolation and that it needs to be part of a bigger debate about how the organization is viewed in the marketplace. This is explored in Chapter 3: Becoming an employer of choice.

As with any significant people development issue, the role of the senior team and the management infrastructure is critical in the development of talent. We explore the impact of leadership style on the retention of talent in Chapter 4: Supporting the new leaders.

Many HR people spend most of their time focusing on the immediate, responding to requests for resources to meet current demands. Rarely is this addressed as a coordinated and coherent plan of talent development. It is also critically important that it is on the agenda of the leaders in the business, not just once in a while but with a consistent ongoing focus. We suggest how this may be achieved in Chapter 5: Future proofing the organization.

Talented people are different. What do they really want? Instead of seeing them as a commodity, we want to focus on them as individuals, to see the world through their perspective. To understand what it feels like to be talented, including the challenges and the advice that they would give to organizations about how best to develop them and support them, we explore this in more detail in Chapter 6: Talented people: what are the motivators and drivers?

As mentioned earlier, talented people are often looking for more than just a job. We explore how to support the growth of talent in Chapter 7: How to create the right environment for talent to thrive. In Chapter 8: Creating a talent pool, we look at talent and employability and how to manage the implementation of the talent development process.

One of the drivers for talented people is being involved in interesting work. In terms of organizational innovation, being able to generate new approaches, new ideas and new ways of doing things is becoming increasingly important. Therefore in Chapter 9: Developing thought leadership, we explore some of the underlying principles around thought leadership and how you can help to develop a 'thinking' organization.

In Chapter 10: The future for talent development, we draw conclusions from our research, the case studies and the personal views and we explore what may be the future trends in talent development.

In Chapter 11: Talent – a personal view, and in the case studies at the end of the chapters, we have tried also to identify other writers, individuals and case study companies who, like us, believe passionately that the war for talent can be won. We invited them to share their campaign stories and give us inspiring examples of how you can achieve real change in the way you attract, engage, develop and retain talent. We hope our findings will add to the debate about some of the best ways of developing talent.

Finally, as mentioned above, Chapter 12: The basis of our research gives you information about our research to date, which is ongoing. Every time we meet with a talented person, or work with an organization, we identify new dimensions in the talent debate.

KEY PRINCIPLES

We have, however, identified some key principles in our research. Talent development is not about a special few people. Real talent development is about playing to everyone's strengths. It is about championing diversity and encouraging creativity and innovation. But above all it is working to create an environment where the organization buzzes with energy and people have a sparkle of anticipation when they enter their workplace. Here are some conclusions:

▌ Be committed to and respect all your human capital.

▌ Encourage and develop diversity within your workforce.

▌ Don't just pay lip service to the concept of talent management.

▌ Focus on it and demonstrate your commitment from the very top of the organization.

I Recognize the importance of your employer brand. Demonstrate your values and brand in the way you conduct your business and develop your people.

I Create an honest, positive and thinking environment.

I Develop your emotional intelligence.

I Be committed to identifying and recognizing talent at all levels in your organization.

I Give individuals freedom to innovate, generate ideas and receive feedback.

I Develop coaching and feedback processes throughout your organization.

I Create an environment that attracts potential employees to want to come and work for you.

I Create internal forums that allow for healthy debate and discussion.

I Encourage flexible and imaginative patterns of employment.

I Ensure your management structure is developing new talent and creating a coaching and learning culture.

I Encourage all employees to be committed to developing your talent pool.

I Make an ongoing commitment to your community in deeds as well as donations.

The reason why we wanted to write this book was that we believe that many organizations do not really understand talented people. We also believe, from years of research with talented people, that while they are different, they are not necessarily difficult and that organizations could, with the introduction of some very common sense strategies, make some significant changes that could enhance the lives not only of talented people, but of all employees.

Talent is not a rare commodity — it is simply rarely released. So this book is as much an exploration of what inhibits the release of talent, as it is an introduction into how you and your business may be able to create a climate where talent isn't exceptional — just normal!

This was our view at the start of our journey. As we reach the end of our initial research with the completion of this book, we have met some very special people who have shared their views about talent and we have identified organizations who have not just focused on talent, but who have embraced its development with a passion and commitment. We thank them all for their contribution, for without them this book would not have been written.

As for us, this isn't the end of our journey. We continue to research into talent, we are developing a series of profiles to identify individual talent, organizational readiness to create a talent culture, and we continue with our consultancy assignments, reviewing approaches to talent and designing ways of building a talent culture. We would love to hear your experiences of talent, what has worked, what has proved more challenging and how you have attracted, retained and developed talent.

Writers often seek to achieve change, to influence, to make something happen, so that they can look back and say that book, that article, made a difference. Easy to say, much harder to achieve. As readers, you can choose to ignore or challenge what you read. What we hope is that you will find in this book information, knowledge, or case study examples that will have a resonance with you and will inspire you to want to try and make a difference. Not just for the talent in your organization, but to also make a difference to your own learning, your achievements and the fulfilment of your own ambitions, dreams and aspirations.

Footnote

There is a logical sequence to the chapters but experience has shown that talented people can also be unconventional, enthusiastic and risk-takers. So use the book in the way that suits you and your style of learning, work through it sequentially, dip into it, or start from the back! Whichever approach you use, we hope you enjoy reading it.

1

What is talent?

We can only wonder at what makes someone talented. However hard we try to define it, talent remains almost indefinable. We gather words together, seeking a definition. Talented people are creative, self-confident, self-starters, edgy, resilient, entrepreneurial, intellectually flexible, opportunistic, unique and different, but in reality the list is endless.

We watch in awe as sports people, musicians, artists and writers create performances, concerts and works that amaze and inspire us, but we don't really understand the internal programming that drives them and gives them such raw talent.

We see gifted children, students and employees display intuition, creativity and imagination in their day to day studies or employment, and we know they are different. We may not be able to describe it accurately, but we recognize it when we see it.

We look at ourselves, we question our achievements and we ask ourselves 'Are we talented?' No one ever quite knows for sure. What one person describes as brilliant, another can question and ridicule, so no wonder then that many people are reluctant to acknowledge that they might be talented.

SO WHERE DO WE START?

Our starting premise was to try to identify some working definitions of talent:

'Extraordinary individuals certainly make life more interesting. They add to our pleasure and mental nourishment, though sometimes also to our travail... Certainly there are rewards for extraordinariness – at times extraordinary people are treated as if they were important; perhaps more significantly, they come to feel that they have made a difference during their lifetimes and perhaps for posterity. But the costs of embarking on a life marked for extraordinariness are considerable. To begin with, one must have enormous dedication to one's domain and mission...The extraordinary individual is also perennially at risk for pain, rejection and loneliness. Most innovators and innovations are not well understood or appreciated at the time of their launching.'

Howard Gardner, *Extraordinary Minds*

In contrast the *Concise Oxford Dictionary* defines talent as 'a special aptitude, or faculty', which, while accurate, somehow doesn't really do justice as a description of our most talented people.

This rather ordered definition also contrasts with some of the descriptions that we found in our research:

'A buzz! How to grasp initiative, inspiration, drive to succeed, resilience, high self-motivation, articulation, self-belief, natural leadership.'

'Someone can be talented and totally self-centred, which I believe undermines their talent and eventually can lead to their downfall. On the other hand, I believe true talent is when [people have] the flexibility to be self-centred and aware of the impact they have on the world at the same time so that they are best able to use their talent for the "common good" rather than egotistical ends. These are some of the words that come to mind: self-belief, identity, natural ability, commitment, passion, resilience, energized adaptability, perceptive.'

'Talent is anything! Absolutely anything, done well (and done well by the person's standards, not comparative to others) and enjoyed. Cleaning the loo through to building the Great Wall. And probably my view is that talent is not the obvious ones... it's more the cleaning of the loo, being able to cook a meal on a sixpence, bringing up a family etc. That's the best talent. Anything and everything is talent to someone!'

'Focus, achievement orientation, self-insight, emotional resilience, confidence, optimism, pragmatism, self-belief, spirit of adventure.'

'Confidence in their ability, proven past success, enthusiasm, commitment, initiative, willing to walk alone and happy to meet with others on the way. General risk-taking is not a problem. Consistent results regardless of the circumstances. Difficult to manage and may not be a team player, if more talented than those around them. May get easily frustrated at others' lack of ability or flexibility.'

'A talented person is someone who has ability above others and does not need to try hard to use it. They excel with ease and grace. A talented person has a certain aura in their ability that others wish to emulate and from which lesser mortals draw inspiration.'

WHAT IS TALENT MANAGEMENT?

We would prefer to call it 'talent development' as it is actually quite difficult to manage talent. Talent slips and rolls around an organization, and often before you realize it, it has disappeared out of the door.

Organizations often try to set up talent management processes, but real success comes when you engage with the hearts and minds of individuals. The organizations that achieve most success with this are those where the vision and values of an organization are aligned with the individual. We give examples of those who are working towards understanding talent in our case studies.

Fundamentally, talent development needs attention to make it happen. It also needs a holistic approach, like customer service, quality standards and health and safety. You cannot just give the responsibility to one person and hope that it will happen. There has to be a belief and a commitment to make it happen from the CEO and the executive right through line management to the newest recruit.

Organizations can convince themselves that talent management is being carried out when they create a system to define the steps, or outline a process to manage talent. However, talent development only happens when you create a culture based on shared values and beliefs, where thinking and feeling emotions are engaged and the leadership demonstrates its commitment through its behaviour and attitudes.

Individuals joining an organization need to feel that they are valued and that their contribution will make a difference. It is easy to say that this is happening, but far harder to have concrete evidence of its application.

In any discussion about talent development, or development of 'high potentials' it is important first to emphasize the development of all individuals. No organization should focus all its attention on developing only part of its human capital. What is important, however, is recognizing the needs of different individuals within its community.

In the search for an effective process for developing talent, most organizations recognize the need to do it differently. However, the challenge is often to identify how and where to start. One of the underlying principles of this book was that we wanted to identify models and case studies that provide relevant examples of how to move from the theory to practical application. Where appropriate at the end of each chapter we have included practical checklists for potential action.

We also recognized that talented people do not necessarily fit into an easy system of classification. People are talented in many ways. Some may have a particular aptitude for doing something, which may be primarily skill based. Others may be gifted artistically, and yet others may demonstrate their talent in more outrageous ways and may be seen as maverick in their approach to life. We have worked across the whole spectrum of capability and have tried to draw conclusions that are applicable in the broadest context of talent development.

THINK ABOUT THE BIGGER ORGANIZATIONAL PICTURE

One of the most comprehensive and well-respected summaries of the key issues around talent is contained in _The War for Talent_ by McKinsey & Company consultants Ed Michaels, Helen Handfield Jones and Beth Axelrod.

Based on five years' in-depth research surveys of 13,000 executives at more than 120 companies and case studies of 27 companies, they identified five imperatives that companies need to act on if they are going to win the war for managerial talent and make talent a competitive advantage. These are summarized as:

1.   Creating a winning EVP (employee value proposition) that will make your company uniquely attractive to talent.

2.   Moving beyond recruiting hype to build a long term recruiting strategy.

3.   Using job experiences, coaching and mentoring to cultivate the potential in managers.

4.   Strengthening your talent pool by investing in A players, developing B players, and acting decisively on C players.

5.   Central to this approach is a pervasive talent mindset – a deep conviction shared by leaders throughout the company that competitive advantage comes from having better talent at all levels.

The War for Talent was written in 2001, and yet in 2006 many organizations have failed to adopt what is apparently a very logical blueprint for success.

One very fundamental question for organizations is 'Where does talent fit in your people development agenda?' This question, while apparently simple, can result in some surprisingly complex answers. The reason for this is as follows. Talent may not necessarily fit neatly into an HR agenda. Organizations have established processes for recruitment, performance management, training/learning and development and reward. Then one day someone, often higher up the organization, perhaps at a board meeting, raises a question. 'What are we doing about creating the people who are going to succeed us?' Or equally, someone says 'Why are we losing so many staff?' Or 'What are we doing about leadership?' Or 'Didn't we used to have a graduate programme?' Sometimes it is a result of a new HR director, or head of learning and development arriving and putting talent on the agenda.

Any debate about talent cannot just focus on one group of people. It is about the bigger organization, and in this context we have to be more radical. Organizations need to identify what type of organization they want to be. In the last decade there has been a real growth in SMEs, employees are becoming more challenging, and there are real issues about retention.

In a *Fast Company* article (2001), Bill Breen discusses some of the research of Richard Florida, founder and director of the Software Industry Centre at Pittsburgh's Carnegie Mellon University. Using focus groups, interviews and an eclectic array of demographic data, Florida plotted the sociological factors that enabled cities to attract human capital. In the battle for talent, Florida argued that location was supplanting the corporation. Chief among his findings:

'In an insecure, temporary, free agent-dominated world, the crusaders of the new economy increasingly take their professional identities from where they live rather than from where they work. Florida had a similar message for people who work in high-tech and other hyper-growth professions. Place is just as important as salary and career opportunity. In his focus groups and interviews, virtually every person who made a job-based decision to relocate, but neglected lifestyle factors such as recreational and cultural amenities said that they moved again shortly after.'

One of the crucial factors of Florida's research is loyalty. Breen talks about the '"Organization Man" of the 1950s, who worked for a company for life, and his social behaviour was defined by that vertical organization'. He compares this with the view of one of his students: 'My work is a series of projects. My life is a series of moves. My parents had institutions that they connected to. What can I connect to, my community.'

In *High Velocity Culture Change*, Pritchett and Pound (1994) argue that you should bring in a new breed of employee:

> 'Break out of your conventional selection/placement practices and find people who clearly do not fit the existing corporate mould. Recruit purposefully. Hire very selectively. You want pistols, hot-blooded people bent on making their mark. Not mild-mannered, conforming types who will succumb to the awesome power of the existing culture. Organizations tend to hire in their own image, and you must avoid that trap if you plan to restaff in ways that reshape the culture. The idea, again is to overcome insularity, insider arrogance, and the "not invented here" syndrome. Hire mavericks. Renegades. Some Walt Disney types with creativity and natural curiosity. Seed the organization with people whose overall make-up will drive the culture in the right direction. Bringing in a new breed makes a powerful statement about the kind of behaviour it will take to survive in the culture that is coming.'

In *The Circle of Innovation*, Tom Peters (1997) talks about becoming a 'Connoisseur of Talent'. He examines the approaches that a number of people have taken to hiring talent. He describes Steve Jobs, CEO of Apple and Pixar, and his recruiting approach, saying that Jobs hires people with 'intriguing backgrounds' and 'extraordinary taste', 'for example, artists, poets and historians'. Their magic, according to Jobs, is that they have exposed themselves to 'the best things that humans have done and then brought those things into their projects'. Peters describes how Jobs' original Macintosh team was a 'marvellous mix of artists and engineers. Their aesthetic interests were as strong as their techie interests.'

Peters goes on to discuss Howard Gardner's 'multiple intelligences' (we discuss this in more detail Chapter 6) and suggests that while each of the multiple intelligences is important, 'most recruiting, selection and promotion processes focus on just one of them, logical – mathematical. What a waste!' In support of his statement 'Hire for attitude, train for whatever', he also cites a quote from Marcy Carsey, the founder of The Carsey–Werner Company:

> 'There's always a force at work toward non-diversity... whom are you relying on to execute ideas, whom are you relying on to come up with the ideas?... There's always a push toward uniformity that we have to struggle against... Most people's natural instinct is to hire people they

are familiar with, that sound like them... We have to fight against that all the time in ourselves, as well as in the people whom we hire, who are then going to be hiring other people. We reach for the broadest spectrum of points of view and personalities and backgrounds.'

In Ricardo Semler's *Maverick* (1993), he describes the working conditions within Semco, where huge loyalty has been built up because individual needs are respected and individuals are given freedom. Semler says that he would rather create an environment where people want to come to work than one where they have to come to work, and this is also borne out in the research by Bennis and Biedermann (1997):

'Many working environments are far too serious and lacking in inspiration.'

John Kao, in *Jamming: The Art and Discipline of Business Creativity* (1996), takes up a similar theme:

'When I get together with other musicians for a jam session, the group starts with a theme, plays with it, and passes it around. Suddenly the music lifts off, flies. We all fly with it... It's an explosion of inspiration within art's given universe. No matter how high we fly, we always return with something new, something we have never heard before... Development occurs. We get emotionally involved...'

All this is risky. Unavoidably so: when the alto sax player starts a solo he doesn't know where he is going, let alone how far and for how long. His inner voice – to which the music, other players, the setting, even the listeners contribute – directs him. That is the nature of improvization and companies that aren't willing to take its risks are not long for this fluid, protean, constantly challenging world.

In *Sex, Leadership and Rock 'n' Roll*, Peter Cook (2006) develops the music theme:

'For the last 200 years people have led enterprises as if they were orchestras. Obsessed by the need for order and control in the way work should be organized, they created structures into which people were fitted. This meant that one person (the conductor), held the composer's operating instructions (the score).'

He suggests that this analogy is increasingly out of step with the way that innovative businesses get things done because:

'The CEO does not and cannot know everything required for establishing a top-down strategy. At best they have only some of the sheet music, or even worse may be using an outdated score. They may be better playing than conducting...

These days you find staff who won't follow the conductor's directions. This is more likely if your current staff come from the so-called generation X (people born between 1964 and 1981) and Y (post 1981). These people are noticeably different from the Baby Boomers (pre-1964). They crave change, challenge, hedonism, speed, instant gratification, progression and freedom. They are individualistic and reject traditional forms of leadership based on a command-and-control model. In short they will not be pushed around, even if their bosses think it is good for them. Moreover, they are very aware of their market value and will walk if they think they are not well catered for.'

Finally, an important issue is raised by Brown and Hesketh in *The Mismanagement of Talent* (2004). They challenge the core assumptions that organizations seek to exploit the talents of all their employees. Instead, they suggest more resources are being attached to a small minority of recruits destined for senior and executive management. Their conclusion is that 'many companies have yet to grasp the full implications of mass higher education, or in some cases, the requirements of knowledge-driven productivity. The major problem confronting organizations today is how to educate, select and develop the wealth of talent now entering the job market with close on two decades of formal education.'

They suggest that 'the focus on recruitment and the talents of the few, rather than training the workforce as a whole, also underplays the importance of the work context, and the contribution of all employees irrespective of their position in the corporate pecking order.' They quote O'Reilly and Pfeffer (2000):

'The unfortunate mathematical fact is that only 10 per cent of the people are going to be in the top 10 per cent. So, companies have a choice. They can all chase the same supposed talent. Or they can... build an organization that helps make it possible for regular folks to perform as if they were in the top 10 per cent.'

It is against this backdrop that we begin our journey of exploring talent in the context of the challenges faced by organizations today.

IN SUMMARY

▍ In any discussion about talent development or development of high potentials it is important first to emphasize the development of all individuals.

❙ Talented people do not necessarily fit into an easy system of classification. People are talented in many ways. Some may have a particular aptitude for doing something, which may be primarily skill-based. Others may be gifted artistically, and yet others may demonstrate their talent in more outrageous ways and may be seen as maverick in their approach to life. As Howard Gardner says 'Extraordinary individuals certainly make life more interesting.'

❙ Organizations can convince themselves that talent management is being carried out when they create a system to define the steps, or outline a process to manage talent. However, talent development only happens when you create a culture based on shared values and beliefs, where thinking and feeling emotions are engaged and the leadership demonstrates its commitment through its behaviour and attitudes.

❙ 'There's always a push toward uniformity that we have to struggle against... Most people's natural instinct is to hire people they are familiar with, that sound like them... We have to fight against that all the time in ourselves, as well as in the people whom we hire, who are then going to be hiring other people. We reach for the broadest spectrum of points of view and personalities and backgrounds.'

Marcy Carsey, founder of The Carsey–Werner Company

❙ 'The unfortunate mathematical fact is that only 10 per cent of the people are going to be in the top 10 per cent. So, companies have a choice. They can all chase the same supposed talent. Or they can... build an organization that helps make it possible for regular folks to perform as if they were in the top 10 per cent.'

O'Reill and Pfeffer, *Hidden Value* (2000)

AUTODESK CASE STUDY

What does your organization do to create a culture and climate to encourage the learning potential of all employees?

We attach a lot of emphasis on the importance of culture and truly see it as part of our competitive advantage. Our view is that learning and development are a shared responsibility between the business and employee. This point of view is first shared during hiring and reinforced in orientation. We highlight all that Autodesk offers for development. We also say that it takes two to make it happen.

We believe it is smarter to focus on employability rather than job security in today's environment. So, we try to come up with courses that our employees need now and will need in the future.

With regard to who we train; we believe that by developing our core group of solid performers we can really make a difference for the business. It is also great for people who work here... everyone has access to development.

We are broadening our offerings now so that training is not the only way; more and more, we offer coaching and on-the-job opportunities for development.

How do you attract, engage and retain talented people?

Autodesk is well known as a great company to work for and so word of mouth and referrals bring a lot of people to our door. We are unusual in high-tech in that so many of our staff stay with us for 7–12 years.

We have taken the idea of engagement out of mere conversation and started to measure it, linking engagement to productivity. Our first corporate engagement survey showed high marks, but we are committed to increasing our scores by 10 per cent this year. The divisions have the task and freedom to explore how to make that happen. Overall, we know we want and need to do a better job of career advancement and that will help us with retention.

The culture here really helps us keep top talent. We have a level of flexibility in where people can work; some parts of the business are very virtual. We also have a bias for innovation and need people to bring us the good idea.

How have you managed the ongoing expectations of talented people?

Our staff tend to be creative so you always have to be on the look out for the next challenge. That is not always easy or possible, but it is what our best managers encourage in their teams.

We have had yet another wake-up call about the importance of the immediate line manager in how the employee experiences the company and their opportunity to grow. It is critical that your management staff get how important their role is, how they set the tone, set the stage and sometimes, unfortunately, set people up for disappointment.

We are increasing development of line managers. We already have a mandatory manager curriculum and it would be interesting to test pre-management certification as well.

What are the biggest challenges in managing talent within your organization?

We need to respond to the feedback that we get from our employee survey and our focus groups. And as we get larger and the workforce starts to turn over we need to keep our entrepreneurial spirit alive. There could be resistance to what employees perceive as 'corporate' or HR managed programs. So the questions are: How do we ensure consistency in development programs without stifling creativity and initiative? How do we develop programs that appeal to different age groups and cultures?

How have these been overcome?

HR needs to stay very close to the business and development needs to be 'owned' by the line as well as HR. Keeping in step with the business helps HR stay current with workforce planning – sharing the responsibility means programs are relevant, sponsored and implemented.

What have been the benefits (particularly business ones)?

Using metrics as we did with the Engagement Survey helps demonstrate the linkage of 'HR hobbies' like engagement to actual productivity results.

What measures or processes have you put in place to measure the effectiveness of your talent strategy?

Each division regularly carries out an organizational review to take stock of the talent and skills. We have separated compensation discussions from performance reviews so development has the limelight it should.

The bottom line results are probably our retention numbers, financial performance and employee satisfaction scores.

What advice would you give to others?

Leadership Development Managers, Ann Moreira, says:

> 'Anyone who is an internal working in learning and development is probably dealing with many of the same issues. My advice is to network like crazy with other colleagues in the business... blow down walls, initiate sharing best practices – inevitably it grows the talent pool for everyone'.

About Autodesk

Autodesk, Inc. (NASDAQ: ADSK) is wholly focused on ensuring that great ideas are turned into reality. With over seven million users, Autodesk is the world's leading software and services company for the building, manufacturing, infrastructure, media and entertainment and wireless data services fields. Autodesk's solutions help customers create, manage and share their data and digital assets more effectively. As a result, customers turn ideas into competitive advantage by becoming more productive, streamlining project efficiency and maximizing profits.

2

The strategic role for HR

Is HR valued? HR has for most of its life had a troubled relationship with the rest of the business. A professional in the finance department would be unlikely to suffer as much for his or her profession an HR professional. HR is one of the most misunderstood and (often) misrepresented functions in any organization. Often only willingly consulted when there is a problem, HR may be seen as an internal police force, interfering, lacking in real business knowledge and often the last people to be consulted on major business issues. And yet HR's main rationale for existing is as guardians of human capital. So how do you resolve this dichotomy?

In *The HR Value Proposition*, Ulrich and Brockbank (2005) state the following:

> 'For the last decade, HR professionals have aspired to be the most complete players relative to the core issues of the business, as described in a number of business phrases: business partners, strategic partners, full contributors, players in the business and so forth. These aspirations are appropriate and desirable, but the fact that HR professionals continue to frame aspirations in these terms communicates a continuing concern.'

This theme is continued in a *Fast Company* article by Hammonds, 'Why We Hate HR' (2005). Hammonds constructs a very powerful argument about why HR is viewed so negatively by many businesses:

'After close to 20 years of hopeful rhetoric about becoming "strategic partners" with a "seat at the table" where the business decisions that matter are made, most human resources professionals aren't nearly there. They have no seat, and the table is locked inside a conference room to which they have no key. HR people are, for most practical purposes, neither strategic nor leaders.'

He argues that most human resources managers are not particularly interested in, or equipped for, doing business. He quotes Anthony J. Rucci, executive vice president at Cardinal Health Inc., a big healthcare supply distributor. 'Business acumen is the single biggest factor that HR professionals in the US lack today.'

Unfortunately Hammonds also quotes some fairly damning research about even the core activities of HR:

'In a 2005 survey by consultancy Hay Group, just 40 per cent of employees commended their companies for retaining high-quality workers. Just 41 per cent agreed that performance evaluations were fair. Only 58 per cent rated their job training as favourable. Most said they had few opportunities for advancement — and that they didn't know, in any case, what was required to move up. Most telling, only about half of workers below the manager level believed their companies took a genuine interest in their well-being.'

This is a very real issue for HR, OD and L&D professionals, who, despite all the best efforts of very talented individuals to be heard, or to create a meaningful dialogue, have long struggled with trying to position themselves as interested and interesting partners.

One of the points that many HR commentators make is that HR really should not be treated any differently than any other function. Therefore the argument is that HR should step up to the mark and think about the real value that it adds.

Being invited to take part or persuading others to let you join in will depend on your ability to be seen as adding value.

The HR credibility debate can be highlighted around a number of key issues:

1. First and fundamentally the HR director and head of learning and development need to establish strong relationships with the business.

2. This needs to be cascaded down, with all HR and L&D professionals developing a sound understanding of the business, its overall goals, business strategy and functions. Time must be spent in the business, seeing what happens on a day to day basis

and identifying exactly who are the key stakeholders and their needs.

3. A real and tangible audit of services and products, quality of response, solutions and the expertise of HR staff needs to be undertaken.

4. Conversations need to take place with all business customers on what works, what doesn't work and what needs to be improved as well as predictions for the likely future requirements.

5. Commitment to change must be made and followed through.

6. It is only from this position of knowledge that HR and L&D can really start to build a meaningful relationship with the business.

7. Often if you are part of an OD, L&D or training function you may feel slightly removed from the process of transformation. In some organizations following on the wave created by BPR (business process re-engineering), or perhaps the introduction of a major HR or IT implementation, the people development implications can appear somewhat down the corporate agenda.

8. However, as more and more organizations are realizing that people operate the systems, focusing on enabling the individual within an organization to transform their performance is an important role for all OD, L&D or training professionals to play.

9. Any HR/OD/L&D strategy and vision needs to be built on the overall business strategy and vision. It should complement the business requirements and be based on key deliverables. Every HR professional should create channels of influence in order to keep people development on the corporate agenda. The only way that this will be achieved is to become more proactive and to present people development as an important agenda item for the whole business. There needs to be a two-way dialogue and communication, and a realistic approach to developing people in the context of business growth.

10. HR should be asking 'How do we manage our pool of talent to suit our evolving business need?' This links to ownership of the talent agenda and HR are 'keepers of the people strategy' and, aligned with the business, should be creating an audit tool. 'How much of what we need have we currently got?' 'How much of what we need can be created from what we have

already?' 'How much of what we have cannot be used by us effectively over the next one to three years?' 'How much of what we need is needed from outside — where are they now and how do we attract them?'

If you are invited to be a business partner, this can only really be achieved from a position of engaging with the business properly. One way of achieving this is by researching answers to the following questions:

▌ Do you have a clsear overview of the business vision, values, objectives and key performance deliverables?

▌ Can you accurately describe the current business success of your organization?

▌ Do you know what issues in the business would keep your CEO awake at night?

▌ What are the current challenges being faced by your business sector?

▌ Who are your key competitors?

▌ If you had an opportunity to meet with the CEO and board of your business what would you see as the challenges and opportunities in the business that impact on people development currently?

▌ Have you identified the key 'touch points' where you need to build relationships with the business?

▌ Have you identified the key people with whom you need to partner?

▌ Have you matched them with the right people with the right skills and knowledge?

▌ Have you equipped people with the skills of business partnering?

▌ Have you created a process to map and capture the key requirements from the business and identified the measures of success?

▌ Have you allocated a budget to manage the process, resource the deliverables and to develop the skills of your HR team?

▌ Have you created an overall brand for the function and conveyed this to the business?

▌ Have you streamlined products and services to match the needs of the business?

▌ Have you identified how to create greater autonomy in the business to allow HR to become 'time rich' and allow time to focus on the key deliverables?

▌ Have you considered outsourcing?

▌ Have you developed a system of performance management that allows for individuals to be recognized for their contribution and rewarded accordingly?

▌ Have you created a programme of support for those who underperform in the new environment?

This is quite a significant list of actions, but these are some of the very real challenges being faced by many HR departments today. As well as helping you to become a more effective business partner, addressing the learning opportunities on this list can help with your own continuing professional development.

WHAT ROLES CAN HR EFFECTIVELY PROVIDE?

One very real issue for HR, which cannot be avoided, is how the role of HR will evolve in the future. Many organizations have already cut HR departments as a result of implementing a process of shared services, or alternatively outsourcing some of the more transactional activities. In addition, the role of line managers has been broadened to take on more on-job training or developing their employees through coaching.

In theory this leaves HR with the more interesting and intellectually stimulating work, but in practice for many this only exposes a greater problem for HR in trying to identify what the business actually wants them to do. Ulrich and Brockbank (2005) have added to the debate by suggesting the following roles:

▌ human capital developer;

▌ strategic partner;

▌ functional expert;

▌ employee advocate;

▌ HR leader.

Each role brings a level of specialism and allows individuals the opportunity to gain new levels of expertise. With the changes enforced by restructuring HR it is important for HR professionals to define what they will offer in the future. By working in partnership, HR departments need to identify where they could help the business. Likely areas could be:

- recruitment, working with the business and providers to find the right quality of staff, attracting talent;

- induction, engaging, retaining staff;

- ongoing performance management;

- ongoing succession planning;

- development and assessment centres;

- brokering training, learning and development solutions, including blended learning;

- employee rights, remuneration and benefits, pensions, community investment;

- acting as an internal consultant.

WHAT DEVELOPMENT DOES HR NEED?

One of the biggest frustrations for any professional is not being taken seriously. If you feel you are a 'lone voice', but speaking with wisdom, it is even more frustrating if you feel that no one is listening to you. Like any other influencing situation you need to have a strategy. The first is to identify the reality of your own position.

People who are successful usually have one or more of the following:

- a belief in their own ability;

- personal presence;

- wisdom, knowledge, or particular expertise;

- ability to persuade others;

- status that is respected by others;

- a special something that makes others want to believe in them, be with them, or follow them.

Which of the above do you and your team have? Which ones do you want? Which could you develop? Other areas of development could include:

I enabling skills;

I developing thought leadership;

I business awareness;

I self-confidence and self-belief;

I innovation and creativity;

I growing and managing talent differently to others;

I self-development.

If you believe in yourself it is much easier to convince others to believe in you. Self-belief comes from within. Others can reinforce it, but first you need to plant the seed. Every national sports team develops confidence by encouraging team members to understand their individual strengths. The team coach works to build personal strength, team cohesion and belief in their ability to win. If you are really going to help others achieve their personal learning goals you need to believe in your own ability and you need to develop an inner resilience to help you keep going through difficult times. If you believe in the power of positive thought, you are more likely to be able to support others to develop their own self-belief.

You do not need to start trying to influence the whole organization; focus on the parts that you can influence. Explore the concept of change, read about it, identify case studies of other organizations, talk to colleagues and network with other professionals. Knowledge equals power; seek to influence those around you. Have confidence when talking to colleagues or senior managers, based on the knowledge that you have gained.

Any HR strategy, vision and values will only stimulate interest from the business if they business focused, written in clear accessible language, and seen to be genuinely focusing on the real people issues within the current business agenda.

Take time to explore the content with a trusted colleague from the business, who is prepared to give you open and honest feedback. Don't ever make the mistake of hiding away in the HR department refining your vision, values and strategy, only to find that when you emerge the key players have made a decision to go and play with the ball in a different part of the park.

To end on a positive note, in the _Fast Company_ article mentioned earlier, Hammonds describes a positive role model, Libby Sartain, Chief People Officer at Yahoo, who is developing a model of best practice HR.

> 'Sartain doesn't just have a "seat at the table" at Yahoo: she actually helped to build the table, instituting a weekly operations meeting that she coordinates with COO, Dan Rosensweig. Talent is always at the top of the agenda — and at the end of each meeting, the executive team mulls over individual development decisions on key staffers.'

That meeting, Sartain says, 'sends a strong message to everyone at Yahoo that we can't do anything without HR'. It also signals to HR staffers that they're responsible for more than shuffling papers and getting in the way. 'We view human resources as the caretaker of the largest investment of the company,' Sartain says. 'If you're not nurturing that investment and watching it grow, you're not doing your job.'

IN SUMMARY

▌ HR is really being challenged on its ability to become a strategic business partner. HR is being encouraged to step up to the mark and to think about the real value it adds.

▌ Any HR strategy, vision and values will only stimulate interest from the business if they are business focused, written in clear accessible language, and seen to be genuinely focusing on the real people issues within the current business agenda.

▌ Any HR/OD/L&D strategy and vision needs to be built on the overall business strategy and vision. They should complement the business requirements and be based on key deliverables. Every HR professional should create channels of influence in order to keep people development on the corporate agenda. The only way that this will be achieved is to become more proactive and to present people development as an important agenda item for the whole business. There needs to be a two-way dialogue and communication and a realistic approach to developing people in the context of business growth.

▌ With the changes enforced by restructuring HR it is important for HR to define what it will offer in the future. By working in partnership, HR departments need to identify where they could help the business.

▌ HR should be asking 'How do we manage our pool of talent to suit our evolving business need?' This links to ownership of the talent agenda, and HR are 'keepers of the people strategy' and aligned with the business, should be creating an audit tool. 'How much of what we need have we currently got?' 'How much of what we need can be created from what we have already?' 'How much of what we have cannot be used by us effectively over the next one to three years?' 'How much of what we need is needed from outside – where are they now and how do we attract them?'

The case study below also gives a positive example of how HR can play a significant role in the development of an organization.

PORTMAN BUILDING SOCIETY CASE STUDY

When Ann Elliot, HR Director of the Portman Building Society, arrived in the summer of 2004, one of her first actions was to present the board with a comprehensive 'people strategy'.

As part of the people strategy it was identified that there was a need to drive progress in the following areas:

▌ Upping the Game: in terms of being able to recruit, develop and retain the right people for success;

▌ Driving a Performance Culture: in identifying and growing leaders within the business;

▌ Organization Capability: ensuring that talent is being nurtured and developed in order to create tomorrow's success as well as today's.

In addition it was recognized that if the Portman was to continue to grow at pace then it needed to be clear what 'success' looked like for the leadership team. 'We needed to build capable, well-managed teams, with individuals who have the ability to lead major projects, or to stand in for their principal lead while they are busy managing that growth. We also needed to attract and develop talent for the organization to fill our future leadership roles,' said Ann.

This led to an overall objective, which was as follows:

To provide a leadership development framework, and a talent management process to deliver future management capability.

In reviewing the current training programmes it was important to acknowledge that Portman, like many organizations, was evolving and the development of leaders for tomorrow will be different from the development offered to the leaders of today and yesterday.

Any programme of leadership development has to meet the needs of the individual as well as the business and Portman had a diverse population of senior new entrants and longer-serving Portman employees, and also needed to grow future talent. It was therefore highly appropriate to review the current provision of leadership and talent programmes to identify a way forward that would support the declared objective of enhancing leadership capability within Portman.

As well as reviewing the learning and development programmes there were a number of other factors to take into consideration in the current state assessment of their leadership development process:

▪ There was not an up to date leadership framework defining what 'success' looks like for the leadership team at Portman.

▪ An experience and knowledge gap had been identified at associate director level and below.

▪ Although there had been some level of feedback using a 360 degree mechanism it had not been built formally into a development centre or a succession planning approach.

▪ Some coaching support had been available but this had been identified and offered on a very individual basis and as part of a private contract with individuals, rather than as part of a growth of a coaching culture.

▪ There had been limited self-development for senior managers, but it had not been part of an overall leadership development plan.

▪ Within the organization structure it had been identified that there was a big step from GBM to AD and historically few had made the transition successfully.

▪ As a result of many of the above factors over 90 per cent of senior managers recruited in the last 12 months were external appointments.

▪ There had been little use of external benchmarking to identify examples of leadership development best practice in other organizations.

- As well as focusing on the development of leaders, Portman equally wanted to undertake a 'current state assessment' of their talent development process.

- There was not a defined talent pipeline, or recognized talent management system.

- There were people who may be recognized as 'talented' but this was not integrated into an overall process of talent management.

- Pre-December 2004 there was no accurate assessment of potential talent in the early years at Portman.

- Equally there had been no external benchmarking of talent.

- Internally there are no criteria for identifying talent and no formal process for tracking talent.

- The only structured succession planning happened at board level.

- There had been few opportunities identified where talented people could broaden their experience to help them progress within the business.

- There had been no systematic follow-up to identify why talented people had left Portman.

- There was limited recognition of what 'talent' means within the context of Portman.

- There had not been an opportunity to formally identify future capability requirements matched against current capability and to recognize the predicted gaps.

- With the introduction of the people strategy there was an excellent opportunity to review the current provision and to build a leadership framework, which more accurately reflected the development needs of future leaders within Portman.

In November 2004 Robert Sharpe, as part of his chief executive review, made the following statement:

> 'We want to be clear and transparent with our people about the drivers for success and the requirement to outperform. Equally we need to recognize and reward those who deliver this performance.

In order to achieve this we need to develop our thinking in the three key areas of leadership, remuneration and performance management.'

For the start of 2005 there was a company-wide launch of an updated performance review system, which was seen as a powerful catalyst for change and began to highlight individual development needs. It was recognized that if leaders were going to meet the business and functional objectives successfully and also demonstrate the required behaviours it would be essential to provide them with a programme of development that builds their capability for the future.

It was felt that the feedback from the performance review process would enable potential leaders with their line managers, or coach, to identify focused learning and development inputs. Equally the development required may be linked to a need for broader work experience exposure, which could be met through project work or role rotation. For many individuals it was one-to-one coaching that had most impact, helping them to develop new behaviours and grow in maturity and stature.

To support this, Portman introduced a coaching programme to support all line managers in both the identification of talent and the ongoing performance review.

They recently held their first development centre, which was very successful in enabling individuals to take time out for their own focused reflection on their achievements and performance to date. They also received one-to-one feedback and development suggestions from the observers from the broader organizational perspective of their behaviour, impact, contribution and career options. Together with the development centre team there was the opportunity to identify areas of growth potential against their current role and future roles.

In terms of the ongoing identification of talent, the following key steps have been identified.

The strategic long-term aims:

▌ to attract more 'talented' people into Portman who successfully progress to senior management positions measured through tracking and retention;

I to reduce the current level of external appointments by 10 per cent to 80 per cent;

I to ensure Portman is recognized as 'best in class' for leadership development and talent management.

In practice this means the following:

1. **Creating the talent pipeline**

   – A process has been agreed for identifying how the talent pipeline could be created. Talent criteria have been identified.

2. **Creating the talent pool**
   The criteria for entry to the talent pool are as follows:

   – flying in role;
   – demonstrating leadership behaviours;
   – demonstrating talent criteria;
   – demonstrating additional leadership competencies;
   – demonstrating creative thinking and idea generation;
   – uniqueness;
   – individuals would be deemed ready for role through personal nomination;
   – line manager recommendation;
   – sponsor/mentor recommendation.

3. **Matching talent to opportunities**
   Other actions that need to be undertaken are as follows:

   – job descriptions/role profiles for all key roles;
   – expected competencies, behaviours, talent factor criteria, experience, background;
   – required performance indicators for the role from the performance review system;
   – accepted deviance from desired timeframe for the availability of roles.

   There is a search and scan process to internally assess individuals from the talent pool against requirements:

   – profiles of internal candidates and performance results;
   – matching of performance indicators with the acquired competencies, behaviours, talent factor criteria, experience, background;

- review deviances from the desired results and potential for development;
- interview desired and potential candidates.

Following this, or simultaneously to search and scan external talent, Portman have created their own accredited recruiter programme to support this process.

- as above a-d;
- in addition to benchmark internal candidates against external candidates;
- to highlight potential other opportunities within Portman;
- to establish Portman's employer brand in the marketplace;
- to build relationships with providers, to track and build relationships with future talent;
- once in role as part of the overall talent development, to track overall progress, set performance objectives, identify development needs;
- next stage will be growth in role, progress to higher leadership levels.

4. **Improving succession planning at executive level and building an appropriate talent pipeline**
    Many of the steps outlined above will lead to an improvement in succession planning, and the building of a talent pipeline, but this process will need to be formalized so that in future it is seen as a priority action.

5. **Maintaining an updated talent list, ensuring that Portman attracts and develops talent to fulfil their leadership roles through feedback and support to talented individuals and proactively managing their careers**
    If the overall objective is met and the key stages outlined are achieved then this is a logical outcome. However, it will not be sustained without attention to the detail of:

    - identification of the talent;
    - support and mentoring of individuals;
    - recognition of the succession paths;
    - coaching and supporting managers in giving feedback;

- managing the performance curve;
- externalizing best practice.

It is clear that the Portman has embarked on an ambitious programme of change, but eighteen months on, an enormous amount has been achieved since the introduction of the people strategy.

'Developing emotionally intelligent leadership, capable of sponsoring the potential leaders of tomorrow will not happen overnight,' says Ann Elliot, 'But by building a team of senior managers who are capable of leading by example, inspiring and developing talent and who are able to give intelligent people permission and freedom to excel, will be a great start to the future development of leadership and talent within Portman.'

About Portman Building Society

Portman Building Society is the third largest UK building society and 13th largest UK mortgage lender. In the five years since 2000, Portman has more than doubled in size. During this period Portman was the fastest growing top ten building society by the three key measures of total assets, mortgage balances and savings under management.

The Society's assets now exceed £16.5 billion and the Society and its subsidiaries employ over 2,000 staff serving 1.8 million members. Currently, the Society has a total network of 146 branches. The Society's head office is in Bournemouth, Dorset and it has an administration centre based in the West Midlands.

Contact details: Ann.Elliot@portman.co.uk

3

Becoming an employer of choice

One of the ways that organizations can attract talent is by becoming an employer of choice, and one way of doing this is focusing on developing its 'employer brand'. Increasingly individuals are thinking far more seriously about aligning their values to an organization's values, and so at recruitment they will also look at what an organization can offer them as well as what they can offer an organization. The messages given through recruitment advertising and the recruitment process often have lasting effects on how an individual might view a company.

In Chapter 10 we give an example of how Rusty Rueff, when he was senior vice president of HR at Electronic Arts, used the internet to create a community of potential employees:

> 'We're operating on the leading edge in terms of creating community through technology. When people hear from us, I hope they think "Wow, I thought you forgot about me. And now you're actually contacting me to tell me something has changed and that there's another opportunity?" I know this sounds really simple, but how many companies treat people like that?'

This is a great example of how an organization can create a bond between itself and potential or current employees. It is allowing the natural behaviours to come to the surface and to build enduring relationships.

'Branding' as a generic term is often assumed to belong to the marketing function. Organizations, however, are realizing that directly, or indirectly, people, not products, deliver most brand promises. In the broader context of employer branding it means the way organizations position themselves externally as well as internally. This will have particular relevance in the way organizations promote themselves in the recruitment marketplace, in the way that they deal with customers. The people offer must match the marketing offer. Corporate social responsibility is also becoming increasingly important.

In its simplest form, employer branding is about ensuring that your people brand matches your marketing brand. In terms of brand management, an aspirational goal for an organization should be that the marketing messages are reflected by the actions of all of the people, at all levels of the business and at all times, in order to deliver the brand promise.

Although employer branding has been around since the early 1990s it finally seems that its time has come as more and more organizations begin to recognize its importance. The biggest challenge in adopting a process of employer branding is ownership, because it is often not clear who should sponsor it, and the responsibility can fall down the middle between marketing, corporate communications and HR. To succeed, it needs an integrated process linking all departments with endorsement from the highest level within the organization. As an aspirational goal it also needs a pragmatic approach to achieve it.

One of the definitions of 'brand' in the *Concise Oxford Dictionary* is 'to impress unforgettably on one's mind'. If we explore that statement a little further, it is clear that building an employer brand is an extension of this definition. Every organization has a brand; the impact of your brand is 24/7, 52 weeks, 365 days every year. Although your building may be closed, its image is open for all to see. Your employees, clients and customers may be talking about their experiences to others. Global communications mean that while one part of the world is sleeping, another part may be awake and the various experiences of your organization will give an impression for better or worse in the minds of the people who matter most.

It is increasingly being recognized that having strong consumer brands is not enough. Organizations need to adopt an integrated approach encompassing:

▌ people;

▌ products/services;

▌ processes/systems;

▌ premises/environment.

In terms of employer branding all four elements above impact on the overall experience.

The most obvious one is people. It is no good giving people a badge that says 'We love to help you' when patently the expression on the face above the badge says something different. Investing in customer care programmes won't work if the management style doesn't encourage individuals to take responsibility for their own actions and really to think about what they personally can do to make a difference.

Fortunes are spent on recruitment advertising, implying that an organization wants 'dynamic, innovative, creative, inspiring people capable of acting on their own initiative', only to find that, once recruited, the organizational structure is stifling, hierarchical and doesn't sponsor original thought. Employer branding also relates to the messages that an organization gives to new employees through recruitment, induction, engagement, development and retention.

Most organizations recognize the need to have good products or services, but it is the interaction between the delivery of the product/service that makes the real impact on the customer's experience. Financial institutions discovered this recently when many of their call centres were shifted overseas.

As well as the importance of people and products, the underpinning infrastructure is equally important. When organizations re-engineer, or when new IT systems are being implemented, little time is allowed to prepare for the impact that this can have on their people. Different departments simply do not communicate, or fail to realize the implication of their actions, and unfortunately HR is often the last to be involved. Equally, organizations may invest in the development of their customer-facing employees, but often do not apply the same principles to supporting the internal customer.

Recognizing the issue of ownership highlighted above, the organizational brand model below is a holistic approach to employer branding. From this one model it is possible to highlight all of the key issues related to employer branding and to identify who can sponsor the development.

ORGANIZATIONAL BRAND MODEL

Our vision

(Where we want to be)

Our values

(What we stand for: our integrity)

Behaviours/competencies/standards

(What we demonstrate daily)

Creating an environment where people want to work

(Develop coaching, feedback, sharing)

Working in partnership

(Employees, customers, suppliers, community and the media)

Communicate the key messages

(Internally and externally, gain commitment to key goals)

Sharing with our competitors

(Best practice)

Rewarding performance

(Real measures that we all recognize)

Measuring our success

(Establish a process to learn and grow)

©The Inspiration Network

EMPLOYER BRANDING IN PRACTICE

Our vision/mission/purpose

Where we want to be

This must be a real statement or statements that people can easily remember and identify with, not just words on a wall. It should be very clearly articulated. A test of its validity is that when asked, each and every employee clearly understands what the business is trying to achieve. Strongly identifying with the sentiment is more important that accuracy in the actual words.

> 'When people truly share a vision they are connected, bound together by a common aspiration.'
>
> Peter Senge, *The Fifth Discipline* (1990)

Our values

What we stand for/our integrity

Like vision, mission or purpose, an organization's values should run deep. The aim should be to encourage everyone to demonstrate the values through their behaviours; this particularly applies at senior level, when more junior employees are looking for role models.

In the current marketplace with increasing competition for talented employees, potential candidates are also trying to identify where the values of the organization are aligned with their own. Daniel Goleman, in his book *The New Leaders* (Goleman, Boyatzis and McKee, 2002), goes further when describing how to motivate employees, saying that:

> 'Getting people to really embrace change requires attunement, alignment with the kind of resonance that moves people emotionally as well as intellectually. Strategies couched as they often are in the dry language of corporate goals speak mainly to the rational brain, in the neocortex. Strategic visions and the plans that follow from them are typically linear and limited, bypassing the elements of heart and passion, essential for building commitment.'

Contrast this with the view taken by First Direct:

> 'From day one the business was built implicitly around the idea that employees deliver the best customer service if they are motivated and satisfied with their work and feel that they have permission to do whatever they perceive to be right for the customer.'

As the business grew, a set of values were agreed as the key behaviour that underpins First Direct both internally and externally. They still continually evaluate all their policies and practices against the essence of the brand.

Behaviours, competencies, standards

What we demonstrate daily

This is a key area where cross-functional collaboration is essential. All too often the creation of the 'corporate way' is kept separate from the day to day measurement of individual performance. Employees need very clear guidance on the corporate expectations, eg this is the way we do things, the way our performance is measured; it applies to everyone and ensures consistency. These standards need to be clearly defined, not just 'we promise to do our best', but 'we promise to respond within fourteen days, on time, and to meet identified standards'.

It has to be a two-way process. If an organization wants to attract the best employees it is also important to sponsor talent, to adopt flexible ways of working and to allow people to take responsibility for the success of the organization. Also to be creative, to encourage people to share ideas, to make no assumptions about the way something has to be done but to think about how it could be done differently. One very real issue, particularly for talented people, is time wasting, bureaucracy and trivia. Giving clear guidance on expectations and agreeing the specific details on deliverables means that individuals can really focus on what they need to do. Objectives can be set and work can be completed within a shorter timeframe.

Many organizations adopt anthems, hold motivational events and build inspiring quotes into the fabric of their company. However, this will make little difference unless there is real belief and unity of hearts and minds behind the words. This can only be achieved through a carefully orchestrated and planned process of developing an employer brand.

Create an environment where people want to work

Develop coaching, giving and receiving feedback, sharing

Commitment to people development needs to start at the top of an organization; it is not just an issue for HR or learning and development functions. The leadership behaviours set the tone and expectations for employees. People are smart and talented people are even smarter. They will not be taken in by lip service to values. They want to see an active demonstration in the day to day people management of the business.

One of the recent trends in employee development is a recognition that retention of key employees is going to become increasingly important. With reduced resources available, everyone is going to be competing for the same people. Today's younger employees are much more mobile than previous generations.

It's important to encourage managers to be people who make a difference, and to take time to 'know' the people they manage as individuals – to cherish, nurture, respect, value each person and watch those individuals 'grow'. This is the most rewarding aspect of any relationship. To recognize what people are good at, identify their strengths and provide the opportunity for them to use these skills. Managers should empower by communicating, by giving responsibility and the opportunity to be part of decision-making. They should create a support system to give confidence, stability and security, help people to help themselves. Also, it is essential that they engender a sense of fun about life and work.

Technology can support flexible working. People no longer need to be in an office. For many people, freedom to operate is important; their creativity is unlikely to be contained within office hours. Allowing them flexibility and freedom will ensure that you maximize their contribution. New legislation related to work/life balance will mean that organizations will have to adopt a more flexible approach.

Working in partnership: the way forward

Employees, customers, suppliers, community and the media

No person or organization can function for long alone. Working with people, helping others to be successful, building pride and self-esteem, and sharing success are all important components. Equally, building close links with suppliers, encouraging the media with positive news and building links with your local community are positive partnership actions.

Brand loyalty is created in many ways, but essentially it is all based on the relationships that an organization builds with its partners. Corporate social responsibility is becoming increasingly important. Features like the *Sunday Times* 'Best Companies to Work For', Investors in People, National Training Awards, etc all emphasize the importance of these relationships. No business can afford to ignore its standing in the community or with its customers. One company with perhaps the longest tradition is Whitbread, as Ian Anderson, former community investment director at Whitbread, said in *Corporate Fundraising*:

> 'The provision of financial contributions to the community by business will always be important, but will always be of a limited nature. Donations of gifts in time and gifts in kind can add so much to the fabric of the community and can play to the strengths of commercial organizations by using all their resources.'

Communicating the key messages

Internally and externally, gain commitment from others to the key goals

You need everyone to unite behind a common goal. However, you will also need to identify the people who are going to be most proactive. You do not need to call them champions, but in reality they will be the sponsors of employer branding. You need them at every level in the business from the very top to the newest recruit. They need to quietly (and sometimes loudly!) promote positive messages about the organization. Those who understand the total impact of the brand need to support others who are less clear, or who adopt a 'silo' approach.

Identifying talented individuals does not just mean focusing on people who apply for a job; it means clearly inducting recruitment companies and head-hunters into your brand and expectations. It means thinking very carefully about the messages that are given about your brand in advertisements.

It also means sharing key messages with the people that you meet about your business and the opportunities. You need to keep replenishing your talent pool; ideally you want people to come to you. Entrepreneurial CEOs are often passionate about what they are doing, and that passion is infectious. Think about what Richard Branson has done for Virgin and what Jack Welch did for GE... but it shouldn't just rest on the shoulders of a charismatic CEO. The questions people in all organizations should be asking themselves are 'Are our employees acting as ambassadors for us?' 'Are they talking positively to their families, partners and friends about our organization?' 'What are they saying to our customers?'

The 'perceived purpose' of the business has the ability to inhibit or encourage the release of discretionary contribution 'volunteerism', and in this way there is a link between employer and employee branding.

Employees experience every day whether you are delivering what you promise and this will be demonstrated through their attitudes and behaviour. Nothing will destroy a reputation faster than an organization promoting itself as an employer of choice, only to find its employees informally giving out a very different opinion to its customers, or their own family and friends. People want to work for a company that they respect. Organizations that take employee relations seriously will be seeking to engage the hearts and minds of their employees and seeking to attune their dreams with the organization. This attunement should be demonstrated through the way an organization recruits, develops, rewards and retains individual employees.

From the bottom to the top of the organization (and vice versa), open up channels of communication and encourage the giving and receiving of feedback, and, even more importantly, be seen to be acting on this information.

Sharing with our competitors

Best practice

Be proud of your achievements, and demonstrate best practice. Be the organization that others benchmark against. This will have internal spin-offs for morale. Demonstrating your corporate and social responsibility is one way of addressing this issue. Equally, being part of an employer's forum, or network, sharing best practice, being prepared to be involved in the development of shared knowledge and wanting to create an industry standard are all ways that an organization can input into the corporate marketplace for the benefit of all. If an organization wants to encourage discretionary behaviour on the part of its employees, then it needs to demonstrate its own willingness to support activities designed for the greater good.

Rewarding performance

Real measures that everyone recognizes

Performance should be rewarded not just with money, but personal recognition, which is best demonstrated little and often. Create a reward and recognition system that is not just financial.

Individuals do appreciate recognition for their achievements, being thanked for a particular action. Being given extra responsibility, being made to feel part of something special, all are valued by an employee. Financial rewards are important, but other forms of recognition are also motivational too.

One concern that people often have is how their contribution will be measured. Measures are not always shared with individuals. The organization may be using one set of criteria, while an individual believes that they are being measured against another set. This stage is very much linked to the goal-setting stage. Unfortunately, many organizations still have annual appraisal systems that are not linked to the day to day activities of an individual. It is important that clear objectives are set, which are regularly monitored, and that an individual receives feedback and also has the opportunity to discuss their own view of their progress. In a coaching environment this will happen more naturally. Create opportunities to regularly recognize achievements, both individually and in the team. Take time to thank people who have met targets, helped others achieve, or gone out of their way to be helpful.

Review and progress

Establish a process to learn and grow

How often do you celebrate success? Be open about measurement and success factors, never forget where you started, and realize how much progress has been made. There should be a process of continuous improvement. Ask 'What have we learnt?' and 'Where can we innovate?' To prevent a distorted view of the organization, the process should be seamless from the front to back and from the top to the bottom of the organization. The most innovative organizations innovate, accelerate and innovate again. The larger the organization the more opportunity there is to learn from different parts of the business. The collective knowledge within an organization is rarely captured effectively. You will find many examples of reinventing the wheel, if there is not an effective process of data capture and sharing of best practice as well as the opportunity to learn from mistakes in a blame-free environment.

Once employer branding is initiated you will want to build on and learn from the experience. Employer branding does not require huge resources, but what it does need is often a change of mindset. People need to be prepared to learn from the experience, to share successes. All too often people move on to something new before reviewing the experience and sharing the lessons. Success can be celebrated at different stages depending on the size of the challenge. It is all too easy never to celebrate because the goal keeps moving. In reality, the process of employer branding is never completed. Therefore celebrating the small achievements is vital in order to keep individual motivation alive.

IN SUMMARY

▌ The development of an employer brand can be very useful in attracting talented employees. Organizations are realizing that, directly or indirectly, people, not products, deliver most brand promises.

▌ Developing an employer brand can help to create a nurturing culture that enables individuals to give of their best, which in turn supports the organization in delivering its brand promise. As a holistic process it has a dynamic role to play in delivering true competitive edge.

▌ Commitment to people development needs to start at the top of an organization; it is not just an issue for HR or learning and development functions. The leadership behaviours set the tone and expectations for employees. People are smart, and talented people are even smarter. They will be not be taken in by lip service to values, they want to see an active demonstration in the day to day people management of the business.

▌ Identifying talented individuals does not just mean focusing on people who apply for a job; it means clearly inducting recruitment companies and head-hunters into your brand and expectations. It also means sharing key messages with the people that you meet about your business and the opportunities.

▌ It means thinking very carefully about the messages that are given about your brand in advertisements. You need to keep replenishing your talent pool; ideally you want people to come to you. The questions all organizations should be asking themselves are 'Are our employees acting as ambassadors for us?' 'Are they talking positively to their families, partners and friends about our organization?' and 'What are they saying to our customers?'

The following case studies illustrate different approaches to employer branding and are reproduced with permission from HDA, who originally commissioned them.

HSA CASE STUDY

HSA Group Limited builds on a strong tradition as a mutual cash plan provider since 1922. Over the past five years however, HSA has diversified to becoming a wider healthcare service provider. It now provides cash plans, private medical insurance, and occupational health to corporates, individuals and families through its separate businesses – HSA, LHF, HealthSure, BCWA and Adastral – located UK-wide. As a mutual, HSA Group does not have any shareholders and exists purely for its customers; its employees are part of that customer base too. HSA Group therefore spends time to encourage and motivate staff through various activities and programmes as well as offering great benefits and flexible hours. Because of this HSA Group was awarded 13th position in the *Sunday Times* 'Top 100 Best Companies to Work For' competition.

The HSA Group developed its employer brand in line with its corporate branding and values over the last four and a half years. The values are based on openness, honesty and integrity built within a spirit of community. To HSA, community spirit means employees, customers, suppliers, as well as the larger community within which they operate. Their relationships are built on collaboration and teamwork and they want to build adult and long-term relationships with both their employees and customers.

There has been collective ownership from Des Benjamin, their chief executive, and the board to drive the process forward, but equally employees are encouraged to be proactive and to put their own ideas forward. The customer brand and the corporate brand are seen as primarily being owned by the senior marketing team. However, this team works closely with HR and the line managers to ensure that all employees are living and breathing the brand in providing the customer experience.

The HSA Group has linked its values into its performance appraisal systems and objectives at all levels of the business. Employees are encouraged to recognize that how you deliver the service is as important as what you deliver. In addition, there is ongoing recognition and reward for employees who are identified as offering exceptional service and being good role models. Any employee can nominate them. The reward may be a personal letter, gift vouchers, nights out, or special day events. They believe in the old adage of 'catching people doing right'. Equally, they are not afraid to use the ultimate sanction of dismissing people who, after the correct process of support, are not willing to demonstrate the espoused values.

They are also committed to CSR and devote around one per cent of their annual turnover to healthcare related charities. They also encourage employees to work with charities in their local communities. One recent example was 'Fly the Children', where over one hundred autistic children and their carers were given fights in light aircraft. Staff from across the organization were involved in the event and participated in the logistics of organizing the children and their carers.

The measurable benefits to the business are that customer satisfaction levels are increasing, as is retention. In empathy audits staff are connecting more effectively both internally and with customers and there are positive results from their employee opinion survey. In addition they have also been recognized in the *Sunday Times* 'Top 100 Companies to Work For' over the past three consecutive years, including the top awards for employee well-being for 2005.

Like Virgin, HSA is a rapidly growing and devolved group and feels that it is crucial that as the organization grows, new employees and associated businesses understand how the business has evolved and the underpinning values. One of the key statements for employees is 'Be Yourself', encouraging employees to make use of all of their associated life and social skills as well as their specialist skills.

Overall the company has a commitment and conviction that what it is doing is right, but it also recognizes that the path will evolve and change. When asked what advice they would offer to others, Mark Day, director PMI and HR at HSA, stated 'There is a lot of talk about the need for empirical data but we believe that organizations should start when intuitively it feels right rather than hold back and wait for demonstrable business results.'

VIRGIN CASE STUDY

With a focus on planes, trains, finance, soft drinks, music, mobile phones, holidays, cars, wines, publishing and bridal wear, Virgin is one of the strongest brands in today's global marketplace. It has ndertaken a number of key steps to protect and strengthen its employer brand.

The company ethos is established right at the centre of the group of companies with commitment from Richard Branson and the board at Virgin Management Ltd – VML (known as 'the home of Virgin'). They have a group brand and marketing team which regularly consults with marketing, customer service, and people and internal communications directors around the Virgin Group, helping ensure that brand values and messages are translated through to the day to day actions of all employees.

Virgin is a rapidly expanding group, both in terms of range of product and service sector and also on a global scale throughout five continents. To meet the challenge of consistency in the brand ethos, particularly relating to new start-up businesses, Virgin Management Ltd have created a brand toolkit, which includes practical guidelines to enable all Virgin businesses to understand clearly what it means to be part of that brand. Additionally, all new employees are given a starter pack highlighting the benefits as well as explaining the ethos of the company.

Also in the pipeline is a 'people toolkit', designed to support people directors in understanding what the company stands for as an employer, how it operates as regards its people processes and what it expects its employees to do to demonstrate the Virgin way (particularly in smaller start up companies). These guidelines cover recruitment, induction and engagement, as well as the ongoing development of employees, and are being developed primarily by the 'people team' at VML. Overall, the brand team are responsible for monitoring the day to day practical application of the brand throughout Virgin, but everyone has responsibility for delivering the ethos.

One of the outstanding features of the brand is to encourage people to demonstrate 'Virgin' behaviours and to reward staff for providing service over and above what customers might expect. Virgin has an annual event celebrating the Employee of the Year and there is ongoing recognition through 'Stars of the Month' initiatives. Employees also benefit from extended learning and development, which develops understanding of what is expected in their different roles. One fundamental of this is being personable and 'noncorporate' in the manner they approach customer service. Virgin want to encourage people to engage with their customers in the most natural and helpful way. To this end, staff in their call centres are specifically trained to focus on the human side of their job and are encouraged to work within broad guidelines rather than directly from a script.

In many Virgin companies, the brand ethos and associated behaviours are included within their performance management systems. In general, however excellent someone might be in their technical field they still need to demonstrate the right way of doing things and, as such, show more that just competence in their role. Virgin also applies this principle to its recruitment process, seeking to recruit 'Virgin' people rather than individuals who are just technically adept. Although the brand provides a framework within which companies operate, Virgin companies create their day to day working practices on a largely autonomous basis with each company individualizing its processes under the brand umbrella. This helps allow the group to meet the challenge of maintaining a single identity whilst operating competitively in a variety of business sectors.

Virgin, like HSA and Whitbread, also has a high level of commitment to CSR and has a variety of measures to ensure that it listens to its staff and lives up to its promise to its customers. It also has a charity, Virgin Unite, which runs a number of charitable initiatives as well as creating and supporting Aids, TB and malaria projects in Africa.

In the spirit of Virgin, all employees have access to a range of attractive benefits and discounts from across the Virgin Group. International secondments can offer staff the opportunity to travel to different parts of the world, and socially there is a calendar of events ranging from festivals held at Branson's house to five-a-side football tournaments.

Despite Virgin's obvious success, there also challenges. One very real challenge relates to public perception of the group as a fun brand to work for, as this can sometimes lead to potential or new employees feeling that they will have an easy ride working for a Virgin company. In fact, Virgin employees work very hard and in some businesses areas, for example Virgin Rail, or Virgin Money, there are strict regulatory procedures that have to be observed. Virgin also recognizes the importance of keeping its overall reputation as an employer of choice in the marketplace, and is determined not to rest on its laurels as more employers recognize the importance of employer branding.

Being protective of its brand, Virgin also uses a whole variety of data-measurements to gain feedback on its performance with its end user. These include suggestion boxes on its website, customer feedback, mystery shopping as well as rigorous follow-up on personal letters written to the company. It also undertakes exit interviews to determine why employees might be leaving, and importantly also encourages talented employees to return. One recent measure introduced by Virgin Mobile involved sending ex-employees a packet of 'forget-me-not' seeds with a note inviting them to return if their new role turned out to be less than satisfactory.

One of the challenges for any organization is identifying the business positives of adopting a focus on employer branding. However, in Virgin's case there are some very real and tangible benefits. It has identified that its staff turnover is lower, its employees are more productive and, interestingly, although its remuneration may not be the industry highest, it attracts and retains high-calibre employees who select Virgin as a lifestyle choice and who identify with the company ethos and values.

For other organizations seeking to develop an employer brand, Catherine Salway, Group Brand Manager at Virgin Management Ltd, offers the following advice:

> 'Don't over-hype the organization or try to impose a corporate brand onto individuals by aggressively marketing a process of employer branding. We employ brilliant people so we nurture a culture which allows us to deliver on our values whilst still respecting their individuality. The focus should be on what we can do for them as much as what employees can do for us. Then we have a fighting chance of delivering to our brand promise.'

4

Supporting the new leaders

Based on all our research and the feedback from our questionnaires, one unquestionable fact emerges: leaders have a highly significant role to play in the sponsorship of talent. The relative importance that is attached to people development in the agenda of the CEO and the executive board meetings sends very strong signals to the rest of the organization.

Talent is not just an issue for the HR department. In our case studies it is very clear that the companies that have succeeded in attracting, engaging and retaining talent have done so because of a company-wide commitment to its development. Many of the organizations' top management have invested considerable amounts of time in mentoring talented employees both formally and informally.

As our research has shown, receiving positive feedback, and having senior people showing an interest in their ideas and personal development are very important factors in why talented people stay with an organization.

Communication is equally important. Talented people are often prepared to wait for the right role if they are kept informed. What they find much harder to cope with is their talent passing unrecognized, or line managers refusing to put them forward for promotion because they want to keep the talent in their own department or division. Increasingly organizations are building into line managers' performance management criteria the need to identify and sponsor talent.

HOW DO THE BEST LEADERS LEAD?

Intuitively, great leaders have a knack of building relationships in a very natural way. When they do achieve this, they inspire great loyalty. Some of our case studies are from younger organizations where the leadership style is more inclusive and where there are not traditions of leadership style to overcome. Leaders enthuse others about joining their organizations and the companies have often grown organically, based on the values and beliefs of the founder members.

In *The New Leaders* (2002) Goleman, Boyatzis and McKee paint a persuasive case for the need for emotionally intelligent leaders. They suggest that at 'built to last' companies, which have thrived over decades, the ongoing development of leadership marks a cultural strength as well as the key to continued business success. At a time when more and more companies are finding it difficult to retain the most talented and promising employees, those companies that provide their people nourishing development experiences are more successful in creating loyal employees.

Goleman et al say that 'people can and will change when they find good reason to do so'. Increasingly they suggest the best leaders lead:

> '...not by virtue of power alone, but by excelling in the art of relationship... Such leaders have a knack of attuning to their own sense of what matters and articulating a mission that resonates with the values of those they lead. These leaders naturally nurture relationships, surface simmering issues, and create the human synergies of a group in harmony. They build fierce loyalty by caring about the careers of those who work for them, and inspire people to give of their best for a mission that speaks to shared values. An emotionally intelligent leader does each of these at the right time, in the right way with the right person.'

Reading the paragraph above again, you may very well be wondering where such leaders are working, or where these wonderful organizations are where employees and leaders alike are passionate about shared values. Although Goleman and his co-authors build a compelling argument, in reality, really great leaders are in comparatively short supply and this is not a new phenomenon. Ask any group on a leadership programme to name great leaders and inevitably the same names appear; some are historical icons such as Gandhi, Winston Churchill, or the better known business leaders such as Jack Welch, or political leaders like Kennedy. What they rarely do is name their own CEO, or any of their senior managers.

Marcus Buckingham, in The One Thing You Need To Know (2005), poses the question 'What do great leaders actually do and what talents do you need to do it?' At the end of his chapter about great leading, he suggests that 'Effective leaders don't have to be passionate. They don't have to be charming. They don't have to be brilliant. They don't have to possess the common touch. They don't have to be great speakers. What they must be is clear.' He talks about human universals (our need for security, for community, for clarity, for authority and for respect) and asserts that our need for clarity, when it is met, that 'is the most likely to engender in us confidence, persistence, resilience and creativity. Show us clearly whom we should seek to serve, show us where our core strength lies, show us which score we should focus on and which actions must be taken today, and we will reward you by working our hearts out to make our better future come true.'

In *Presence* (Senge, Scharmer, Jaworski & Flowers, 2004) Senge states the following:

'In a world of global institutional networks, we face issues for which hierarchical leadership is inherently inadequate... We see this all the time as we work with CEOs of even global corporations. It's easy for people on the outside to greatly overestimate their power. I remember one man saying half jokingly that he always imagined that when he finally made it to the top of the company, he would look under his desk and he'd see these levers he could pull to make things happen. He said that it was a sobering experience to finally get to look under the desk and find that there were none... What distinctive power does exist at the top of hierarchies is usually skewed toward power to destroy rather than power to build. In a few weeks, a CEO can destroy trust and distributed knowledge that took years to build. The power to wage war is far greater than the power to wage peace.'

In the same book Flowers suggests that:

'As models of leadership shift from organizational hierarchies with leaders at the top to more distributed, shared networks, a lot changes. For those networks to work with real awareness, many people will need to be deeply committed to cultivating their capacity to serve what is seeking to emerge.'

In the context of HR leadership, Ulrich and Brockbank (2005) suggest that:

'HR leaders must lead and value their own leadership function before anyone else will listen to them... A well-led HR department earns credibility, and the reverse is also true. HR leaders who do not face up to and implement HR practices on their own turf lose credibility when they present ideas to others. This means that hiring, training, performance management and communication within the HR function must all be top of the line.'

In one of our earlier books, *Managing the Mavericks* (Thorne, 2003), interviewees were asked for one piece of advice that they would give to CEOs. Their common advice to CEOs 'is to get close to your people, give commitment, follow through, don't give out mixed messages, allow communication to come up through middle management, actively seek it, don't allow it to be changed and modified by those who do not want others to hear.'

In our research for this book the same sentiments were expressed. There is a definite belief that many CEOs and senior management are too far removed from the day to day realties of employment. Some of the reasons why talented people leave large corporate organizations either to work for SMEs or to run their own businesses are that they want more immediacy and a feeling of being in control of their own destiny. This may seem like over-indulgence or the growth of a 'me' culture, but many talented people are very driven and they find it incredibly difficult to wait. They want immediate feedback because they want to move on to the next stage, their minds are already well ahead, and they become very frustrated waiting for the wheels of organizational bureaucracy to turn.

WHAT IS THE IMPACT OF LEADERSHIP STYLE ON THE RETENTION OF TALENT?

Daniel Goleman, in an earlier book, *Working with Emotional Intelligence* (1998), quotes a landmark study of top executives who have derailed. The two most common traits of those who failed were:

'Rigidity: They were unable to adapt their style to changes in the organizational culture, or they were unable to take in or respond to feedback about traits they needed to change, or improve. They couldn't listen, or learn.'

'Poor relationships: The single most frequently mentioned factor; being too harshly critical, insensitive, or demanding, so that they alienated those they worked with.'

He contrasted this with star performers:

> 'Superior performers intentionally seek out feedback, they want to hear how others perceive them, realizing that this is valuable information. That may also be part of the reason people who are self-aware are better performers. Presumably their self-awareness helps them in a process of continuous improvement.'

Knowing their strengths and weaknesses, and approaching their work accordingly was a competence found in virtually every star performer in a study of several hundred 'knowledge workers' in a study carried out by Carnegie–Mellon University. The authors of the study stated 'Stars know themselves well.'

Goleman further develops this theme in *The New Leaders* (Goleman et al, 2002), suggesting that the singular talent that set the most successful CEOs apart from others turned out to be a critical mass of emotional intelligence competencies. (See Chapter 7, How to create the right environment for talent to thrive.) He suggests the most successful CEOs spent more time coaching their senior executives, developing them as collaborators, and cultivating personal relationships with them. From a business perspective, he suggests that for those companies where the CEO exhibited EI strengths, profits and sustained growth were significantly higher than for companies where the CEOs lacked those strengths. He also cites the following research:

> 'In a tight labour market, when people have the ability to get an equivalent job easily, those with bad bosses are four times more likely to leave than those who appreciated the leader that they worked for... Interviews with 2 million employees at 700 American companies found that what determines how long employees stay – and how productive they are – is the quality of their relationship with their immediate boss. 'People join companies and leave managers' observed Marcus Buckingham, who was working at the Gallup Organization at the time and who analysed the data.'

In our ongoing research about talent we often ask the question: If you could change one aspect of organizations that would encourage the nurturing of talent, what would you recommend? There is a very strong consistency in the answers, which we summarize below:

> 'Encourage trust and leave people to find themselves.'

> 'Senior managers being prepared to step outside their conventional modus operandi and/or being prepared to tolerate and/or support others to do so.'

'Leadership needs to drive the harnessing of human talent – most companies don't have leaders that understand how to do this.'

'Flexibility – understanding that following the "way we do things here" is a recipe for stagnation.'

'Recognition (not necessarily reward) for the value they deliver.'

'More honest feedback on a regular basis, to encourage and reinforce positive risk-taking.'

'Let people work when and where they think they can offer the greatest potential; it always amazes me that more companies do not let their staff work from home now and again. So much more can be achieved and when they are away from the office and the confines of "its" thinking, they can open their minds to thinking in other ways.'

'I can tell from my personal experience, the one thing that the organization must do to nurture talent is to provide challenge to the individual. Continuous challenge of the individual that stretches him/her to their wits' end is the best "mantra" to nurture talent in the organization.'

'For leaders to think.'

'Regular debate and discussion with managers.'

'A greater acceptance of the need to give people a chance to show what they can do.'

'Perhaps a deeper issue is that organizations say they want to be more creative... but do they really? Creative people are often unmanageable loners; do you really want them in your organization? Ninety per cent of creative ideas are garbage, only 10 per cent are actually worthwhile; do organizations really want their managers wasting 90 per cent of their time? It's like putting on a play which is 99 per cent tedium of preparation and 1 per cent exciting when you actually give the performance.'

'Values. Which is a form of belief. If you believe your people are creative, then guess what. You act that way. Then guess what, they act that way.'

'Personal acclaim and recognition following achievements and results and it doesn't always need to be monetary!'

'Not overloading people with routine or administrative work. Giving them time to dream.'

'The key question I guess is how to motivate people to think differently. This is all tied up with rewards, and in my experience this is vitally related to recognition, which may be evidenced in position, job title, work space and also, but not necessarily, pay.'

'Teach people how to learn, not how to be taught.'

'The recognition that not everyone fits into a particular way of achieving a set goal.'

'Change in hours worked, allowing people to work the time that suited them.'

'Hierarchies reinforce self-importance and status and can crush creativity.'

'Foster an environment in which individuals are valued and talent is exposed, nurtured and allowed to fly.'

What is interesting is the balance between freedom and systems. One of the very real issues in large organizations is tracking people. Very often individuals feel that their talents go unnoticed. Equally, there are very real concerns that the middle management layer hides and diffuses the impact of real talent. This frustrates both senior management despairing of the lack of initiative and potential within their organization, and those new and embryonic talents, who get held back because their views may be different from the accepted norm. This was echoed by one of respondents who recognized that perhaps he hadn't shouted loud enough: 'my reluctance to shout about my talents means that nobody notices'. What he was looking for was 'real appreciation of my worth by people who are interested in me'.

The importance of ongoing conversations was highlighted. This links to Goleman's work on emotional intelligence and the skills set required by managers. 'Clarity around understanding expectations of individuals and matching these to organizational requirements and having a "real" conversation about this.'

In our survey our respondents had a similar perspective. When asked what support they wanted from a line manager, there was remarkable similarity in their responses.

Open and honest feedback was high on the agenda, and there was an important link between freedom to operate and clear goals and expectations. Building of relationships between the individual and their manager is also important, particularly the nature of that relationship. Words used were 'ability to listen, to coach, to offer support coupled with loyalty, trust and integrity. Clear expectations and freedom to get on with it.' Equally, alignment of values now has a much greater emphasis from employees.

HOW CAN HR HELP LEADERS TO DEVELOP?

Importantly, as we and others have emphasized, the HR director, head of learning and development and the whole team must be credible. They must be sensitive to the needs of the business and speak with an authority based on a knowledge and understanding of the business. What is interesting is that in many organizations there is a simplifying of the organizational requirements from HR. Leadership development often consists of sending the most senior leaders away on prestigious external courses, MBAs or business-related events. However, increasingly organizations are questioning the value of this and looking more critically at the relevance of such training. Just because something is well established as a pattern of development does not mean that it is still effective.

Many organizations have adopted a competence-based performance management system. These competences may be generated within the individual organization, but there is often a commonality in language and structure and, once in place, they often only requires fine-tuning. Individual learning plans mean that learning and development is driven through a more personalized route. However, it is important to review all training and development and identify the measurable outcomes. Development centres may have more of a role to play in identifying development that is targeted and focused on individual need, and while this may include attendance on some training programmes it may also be supported by more innovative and different development.

Development plan for new leaders

Lower down the organization there are a number of key steps in developing leaders, which build on some of the activities already mentioned in Chapter 2. If you are developing new leaders, here is a checklist of some of the actions that leaders need to take in their work with their teams. The checklist could be used to build a leadership development programme, or in coaching sessions with leaders. It is based on our experience in working with leaders in organizations and can be used to support a competence-based model of leadership development.

1. To be effective leaders within any organization, future leaders need to understand fully the big picture. As part of this, they need to embrace the overall vision and values in their working with other people. Can they clearly translate this into day to day actions so that members of their team can take ownership and fully contribute? How well do they understand the corporate strategy? How confident are they in discussing this within their team? Can they explain business decisions in the context of the overall business plan and company goals?

2. Successful leaders and team members find ways of working together with the minimum of controls. People need to be encouraged to assume responsibility and work to the limits of their abilities. Leaders need to establish ways of working with their teams so that they give clear direction and trust them to deliver what is required to meet the business objectives.

3. In high-performing organizations, boundaries are deliberately pushed to encourage greater autonomy and freedom to operate. With this approach, however, comes greater responsibility. Ask the leaders if they operate within high controls, or they are able to share responsibility with others.

4. People often have very traditional views of what they think a leader should do. It will take time to help them understand that there are different types of leaders. How can new leaders show that they are understanding, approachable and interested in them? If people feel this, they will respond to it in a positive way. Is the new leader ready to listen? It is important to hear what others have to say. Is he or she open to suggestion? How will he or she show others a willingness to listen to their views, feelings, suggestions and ideas, and value them?

5. Encourage the new leaders to create a culture of effective communication, keeping their teams involved in major events, setting objectives within the overall plan, keeping their team aligned, making everyone's contribution count. Develop clear channels of communication about critical business events, help leaders identify when it is appropriate to talk to their team members one-to-one, or in small groups, to ensure consistent delivery of the message, or for global teams consider video/audio conferencing.

6. Help them to recognize the role that they have in developing others. Encourage them to take time to work with their team to try new experiences, and to take responsibility for their own development; regularly review and support their progress. Ask them how they could become a leader who makes a difference. Encourage them to take time to 'know' the people they manage as individuals – to cherish, nurture, respect, value each person and watch that person 'grow'. This is the most rewarding aspect of any relationship.

7. Coaching is one of the key competencies. Encourage leaders to take time to work with their teams, sharing knowledge, helping

them to develop. Recognize that people learn differently. Encourage leaders to share their expertise, to help members of their teams to grow by taking on new responsibilities, help them to succeed by giving positive and constructive feedback. Encourage leaders to seek feedback on their effectiveness. Help the leaders to develop their skills in coaching; this is one of the very real growth areas in personal development for leaders at all levels in an organization. At a time when attendance on training courses is falling, many organizations are investing time and money in developing an internal coaching culture and training mangers at all levels to be coaches.

8. An important competence for all leaders is to recognize talent and encourage their team members to make the most of their competencies. It is critically important that leaders do not hold back talented people but take pride in developing them. They should provide very real opportunities to involve talented team members in different projects, or short-term assignments. They should champion and be willing to promote the ideas of others and help team members build their skills by building from small to greater responsibilities.

9. Equally, they should take a proactive approach to succession planning, creating an environment where people are developing themselves for moves across as well as up the organization. Where appropriate they should encourage global transfers, and help their team to identify opportunities outside of their region or function. Working abroad can also present another way of gaining cultural awareness.

10. Leaders should be encouraged to create personal development plans for each individual in their team, clearly identifying with them their strengths and development areas. They should work to create opportunities for them to develop new competencies and offer ongoing support, additional learning and coaching opportunities. Equally, encourage leaders to remember to ask their team members informally how their development is progressing once they have started.

11. Encourage leaders to think about how they delegate. Ask them to think about the people that they work with. How well do they know their capabilities? Can they identify opportunities to share responsibilities? Work can be delegated upwards, sideways and

downwards. Delegation really means sharing out work in an equitable and fair way. Encourage them to be creative, not always delegating to the same people, but to evaluate workloads, try to do things differently, and encourage different perspectives. Equally, once they have delegated something they should let people get on with it and trust them. Leaders should be there for support if their team members need it, but let them see the task through to the end.

12.   In terms of recognizing and rewarding individuals and teams, both on results and how they were achieved, encourage them to identify with their team the desired outcomes, to set key milestones, and identify deadlines and how they will measure results. They will need to review progress regularly, and stay focused on the goal, redirecting effort where necessary and keeping the desired outcome in mind when reviewing alternative courses of action. Help them to create strategies to achieve their goals. Although it is important to strive for results, it is also important for them to recognize the impact of their behaviour whilst achieving those results. They should also consider the other members of their team, give them public recognition for their effort and take time to celebrate the team success.

If you are coaching leaders here are some of the questions that you may wish to ask them to consider:

Increasing self-awareness

▌ What do I know about me?

▌ Do I inspire people?

▌ Am I a fair leader?

▌ Do people respect me?

▌ Do I seek the views and opinions of the people that I lead?

Building relationships

▌ How could I modify, change or develop my behaviour in order to encourage and develop others?

▌ Who do I know who is a good role model?

▌ Am I understanding, approachable and interested in others?

Supporting talent

❚ How could I ensure that I help others to fulfill their potential?

❚ How can I sponsor and stimulate other's people creativity both in and out of work?

❚ If you are going to inspire others you need to energize and motivate yourself. Ask yourself, what strategies do I have for achieving a life/work balance?

Making a difference

❚ How do I generate my own personal energy and enthusiasm? What could I do differently?

❚ How could I encourage others to make suggestions about how we could work more effectively?

❚ How could I develop my style of leadership?

❚ How could I incorporate coaching into the way I lead others?

❚ How could we develop a coaching environment?

Communicating effectively

❚ How do I communicate with others?

❚ What do I need to do differently so that others are able to share their hopes, dreams and aspirations?

❚ Am I open to suggestion?

Learning to learn

❚ What do I need to learn in order to help others to learn and develop?

❚ What do I need to do to become a better leader?

IN SUMMARY

❚ Leaders have a highly significant role to play in the sponsorship of talent. The relative importance that is attached to people development in the agenda of the CEO and the executive board meetings sends very strong signals to the rest of the organization.

▌ Feedback from *Mavericks'* research shows the common advice to CEOs 'is to get close to your people, give commitment, follow through, don't give out mixed messages, allow communication to come up through middle management, actively seek it, don't allow it to be changed and modified by those who do not want others to hear'.

▌ Receiving positive feedback, having senior people showing an interest in their ideas and personal development is a very important factor in why talented people stay with an organization.

▌ At a time when more and more companies are finding it difficult to retain the most talented and promising employees, those companies that provide their people nourishing development experiences are more successful in creating loyal employees.

▌ A well-led HR department earns credibility, and the reverse is also true. HR leaders who do not face up to and implement HR practices on their own turf lose credibility when they present ideas to others. This means that hiring, training, performance management and communication within the HR function must all be top of the line.

▌ 'People join companies and leave managers' – Marcus Buckingham.

The case study below highlights some of the approaches that new leaders can develop.

UNIVERSAL MUSIC GROUP CASE STUDY

What does your organization do to create a culture and climate to encourage the learning potential of all employees?

We have a compulsory annual appraisal process. We also carry out a talent review annually, when we meet with senior managers to identify which staff are 'high potential with leadership capability', which individuals have put in a good performance but who are not ready for a move and those whose performance is causing some concern. We look very positively at these people. It may be that they have been in a job for too long, or that they are demotivated. We identify key actions, and put together proposed performance plans. We have a very open system of learning and development, which is published on the intranet. We also encourage people at all levels to go to training events together, for example it would not be unusual for a director and a PA to be on a course together. Equally a number of internal programmes are run by our directors and senior managers.

How do you attract, engage and retain talented people?

Our business is about scouting for talent in the world of music so we are perhaps more used to identifying talent then many organizations. We offer a competitive range of benefits. We have done a significant amount of work over the last three years on our total benefits and rewards package. We have introduced a number of voluntary and family-friendly benefits, and we have plans to develop this further. One very important aspect for our employees is flexibility, and there is scope to build a package that meets their needs. We also give them early responsibility. By their mid-twenties, some talented individuals will be running parts of the business.

Who drives the process and which departments were involved?

The CEO, department heads and MDs of the different businesses are very involved, which keeps talented people motivated. We are proactive in the set up of mini-labels to give talented individuals the opportunity to experience running part of the business.

How have you managed the ongoing expectations of talented people?

We run an executive development programme where we give talented people the opportunity to liaise with the board and other directors, and share in strategic information. We recognize that they are our future. In addition, they have more mentoring and coaching. The music industry is an exciting place to work, but we also stay close to our talented people. Our HR director has regular meetings with senior and talented executives. Not only are they rewarded financially, but we also work with the individual, identifying their strengths and weaknesses, staying in touch with them, coaching and supporting them.

What are the biggest challenges in managing talent within your organization?

Avoiding our talented people being poached is a very real challenge. Internally we have a mix of competitive businesses, so we are able to transfer people to broaden and build on their experience. For example, they could move from marketing in one label to marketing in another label with a different product mix and possible greater challenges. People do return to our business after working elsewhere, often with a broadened skill set. Sometimes they take on a consultancy role. We take our exit interviews very seriously, and we do stress that our door is always open for talented people to return.

How involved is HR with the business?

Our SVP of HR, Malcolm Swatton, is heavily involved in the business. Malcolm is on the board and is involved in every significant business meeting. As HR we have a real sense of what is happening in the business. You could ask us most business-related questions and we would have the answer. Our HR managers have weekly meetings with their business partners who use us as sounding boards. Our courses and workshops are very business-related.

What have been the benefits?

We won both a National Training Award and a 'Special' National Training Award in 2003 recognizing the quality of our development. Our stability index is high compared with industry norms. We featured in the 2003 and 2004 *Sunday Times* 'Best Companies to Work For'. In 2004 we were No. 8.

What advice would you give to others?

Head of Management Training and Development, Mairin Gannon, says:

> 'Stay as close to talent as you possibly can. We keep a close connection with all our talented people; they receive coaching and mentoring from senior members of the business. Another important factor is that HR is closely connected with the business and people expect us to be involved in key business decisions.'

About UMG

UMG leads the music industry in global sales with a worldwide market share of 25.5 per cent, according to the International

Federation of the Phonographic Industry (IFPI). The group's world-wide operations encompass the development, manufacture, marketing, sales and distribution of recorded music through a network of subsidiaries, joint ventures and licensees in 75 countries, representing approximately 98 per cent of the music market. UMG is the No. 1 company in countries that together represent more than 50 per cent of the global music market sales, including the US and the UK. UMG's business also includes music publishing.

Contact details: Mairin.Gannon@umusic.com

5

Future proofing the organization: the 'war for talent'

Today's businesses are used to dealing with the immediate. Where there used to be a five-year plan, now there may be a five-month plan. In today's turbulent times, preparing and living with the unknown is a common challenge. Yet increasingly organizations are recognizing the importance of their intellectual property and their knowledge workers, and the need to engage and retain talent. Even in the more disposable industries where employers are used to high turnover, they are beginning to recognize the cost of recruiting and training staff. As the demographics change, as talented recruits dwindle, organizations are making a more concentrated effort to retain not just talented employees.

The word 'talent' trips easily off the executive and HR tongue in 2006, yet very few people under cross-examination are able to describe what the word means within an organization, let alone describe the relationship between 'talent' and strategy, or excellence, or 'future proofing' the business in terms of competitiveness, or market strength.

Talent and talent management have emerged from within the global organizational language of the past 10 years as an evolution of retention and retention strategies. In short, how do we keep our best people?

The evolution in thinking, however, has been profound. What if your *best* people are simply not good enough? What if the challenges of the next five years are so different from the challenges of the past five years that the talent pool within your organization simply doesn't have the behavioural and attitudinal DNA, let alone the experience, expertise and capability to deliver what needs to be executed within the business?

Talent, therefore, is a lever, a mechanism and an approach that helps keep the organization 'ready' for the future.

We hire the right people, we develop all of our people appropriately, we identify our high-performing individuals at every level in the company and we identify our high-potential people, also at every level of the company.

This enterprise-wide approach to future proofing the organization also requires an honest and forthright ability to identify and own up to the real capability of the organization and its products and services, and the ability to robustly define a strategy that addresses reality in our own organization with that which we believe to be happening in other organizations. Our customers, our competitors and those businesses that currently don't fit into either grouping could have a huge impact on our ability to address the challenges of both groups.

Our business strategy therefore has to address more than a glib marketing exercise represented in vision statements, mission statements and platitudes made to values and beliefs. It has to be an executable and measurable plan of how we move our business from one performance curve to another.

The people plan that delivers the human asset performance should have talent as its heart.

In the past HR has usually been seen as the home of the talent conundrum, ie who is good for now and who is good for the future? No organization and no main board director should let this issue out of their sight for very long. Talent is a 'top team' priority, today, tomorrow and forever. It is a process that is never complete and the work-in-progress nature of the talent dilemma requires authority, responsibility and commitment – not forms, processes and assessment centres.

One of the key issues here is the organization's ability and willingness to 'own up' to the reality of the 'here and now' picture. Most change, OD and talent systems fail because of the organization's desire to 'believe' that things are better than they really are. This self-deceit creates a planning system that creates a direction and a goal but with a plan that 'starts at the wrong place' and is therefore doomed.

The role of HR *must* be not to collude with this – it is essential that HR and the OD group, or the owner/board/executive, need to drive integrity and truth as fast as possible. Anything else simply further undermines the reputation of HR.

So talent is something that requires a shift in leadership thinking, a shift in the behaviour of managers and a shift in the culture and values of the business. It may also benefit from the creation of systems and processes to support the initiative, but that should not make us feel complacent that we have addressed the issue of talent if we have a talent register – that's just a fraction of the journey!

THE WAR FOR TALENT

In the 1998 *Fast Company* article, 'The War for Talent', Charles Fishman interviewed Ed Michaels, a McKinsey director who helped manage the original McKinsey study.

There were a number of very interesting points made. The first was about access to talented people: research in the US has shown that large companies are competing with start-ups for talent. The reason behind this was that people had the potential to make a lot of money, which was certainly the belief behind the original 'dot.com' companies, but also, and perhaps more importantly, that they got the opportunity to be connected to the very top of the company at an earlier age. This is something borne out by our case studies at innocent, Universal Music and Virgin.

In the interview Fishman asked Michaels 'What weapons can larger, more established companies use against start-ups and small companies?'

Michaels suggested that the best weapon that large companies can use is to mimic small companies, to create smaller more autonomous units. They can use their wealth to create more opportunity, but what they have had to recognize is what motivates talented people. In our Universal Music case study they also create opportunities for talented individuals to manage smaller parts of the organization.

Perhaps the most significant part of the article was the identification of the best kinds of recruitment campaigns to attract talent. Michaels suggests that there were four kinds of messages:

1.   'Go with a Winner.' It's for people who want a high-performing company, a company where they're going to get lots of advancement opportunities...

2.   'Big Risk, Big Reward.' The people who respond to it want an environment where they're challenged either to do exceptionally well or to leave – where there's considerable risk but good compensation, and where they can advance their career rapidly...

3.   'Save the World.' It attracts people who want a company with an inspiring mission and an exciting challenge – a pharmaceuticals or a high-tech company, for instance...

4.   'Lifestyles.' This message attracts people who are seeking companies that offer them more flexibility and better lifestyle benefits – such as a good location...

Another important point is the need to develop the organization talent pool. McKinsey mentions this and so did our respondents. As one of them states: 'Keep a continuing sense of what you need to develop for tomorrow as well as to deliver today: develop bifocal vision and have strategies that encompass the long and the short term.'

SO HOW DO YOU FUTURE PROOF AN ORGANIZATION?

First you need to understand what future proofing means and how to apply it. In our model there are three key stages:

1.   The here and now. How many people do we need ? What skills do they need and what are they required to do? Who do we need to retain and engage?

2.   Short to medium term. How many people will we need? What different skills will they require? Who do we need to grow and develop?

3.   Long term. How will our business change? Who are our thought leaders? Who will be able to transfer skills? Who do we need to prepare for the future?

The model, though apparently simple, actually raises some very fundamental issues for today's organizations. Five-year plans for many organizations have become a thing of the past. The rate of change, both internally and in the corporate marketplace, has meant that many organizations operate on much shorter timeframes and as a result there is often a need for HR to become like an emergency rapid response unit. The cry goes out that we need more staff in sales, we need more IT personnel, we need a continual loop of call centre staff because we are failing to retain people. Consequently, planning for stages 2 and 3 above rarely gets to the top of the HR agenda as the organizations are constantly responding to the demands of stage 1. This becomes a very real frustration for those individuals tasked with the role of talent management as many organizations do not really address the issue of future proofing in a coherent and coordinated manner.

Future proofing needs a holistic approach. Although there is a need to focus on retaining and developing the right people, it is also important to coordinate people development with other aspects of future proofing and this definitely means understanding what the business is trying to do. Not just from the sidelines, but as in the example mentioned in Chapter 2 of Libby Sartain, Chief People Officer at Yahoo, where 'Sartain doesn't just have a "seat at the table" at Yahoo: she actually helped to build the table': 'We view human resources as the caretaker of the largest investment of the company,' Sartain says. 'If you're not nurturing that investment and watching it grow, you're not doing your job.'

MAKING IT HAPPEN

In an earlier book, *Coaching for Change*, Kaye Thorne (2004), as part of examining 'Five Principles for Transforming Performance', identified that an important part of any transformation programme is about helping people identify and develop the required competencies to ensure that the right people are doing the right things at the right time both now and in the future.

At the start of the process it is likely there may be three categories of development of the people in the organization:

1. Individual and organizational alignment.

2. Alignment but needing development.

3. Discord.

1. Individual and organizational alignment
   The right people doing the right job at the right time. When working with this group as a coach during a transformation process it will be important to encourage, reward and recognize this group as champions. Ideally, they should also be encouraged to take responsibility for making things happen. Take time to ensure that they are supported in what they are trying to achieve. From an organization or a team perspective they should not be held back because of petty bureaucracy.

   As well as sponsoring this group, they may also need real support to stay motivated as they may become frustrated with the speed of change. For those that can see the way ahead they may feel that others are deliberately holding them back. As a coach, be sensitive to the needs of the whole team but also recognize the needs of this group. Acting as a sounding board, encouraging them to air their frustrations, helping them to develop personal action plans to manage the challenges that they are facing is an important role that you can provide as coach. Encourage them too to support others. Being seen as a star can be a great personal motivator but helping them to act as a guide for others can also be important. It is a delicate balance between giving them a free rein and asking them to act as a role model to help others develop.

2.   Alignment but needing development
     With this group it is important to help them recognize where they need to develop. One of the first tasks is to think about the role and to identify if they need to change roles or whether they need to develop new competencies or behaviours. Using profiling tools and competence mapping can be vitally important to identify where the elements of mismatch are occurring. Although this will take time, it is an important part of the transformation process and it is important to the individual as well as the organization. If the role specification has been clearly defined then this could be a good starting point. If this is coupled with an accurate assessment of an individual's competence then as a coach you can work with them to help them identify the growth areas.

     For some this will mean that they need to develop new competencies, for others it may mean that they need coaching to identify the new behaviours that they need to develop. The people in this development category need to identify where the gaps exist and to assess their willingness and motivation to change. This group will need ongoing support, as very little in a programme of transformation can be based on the assumption that once it is set up it will happen. Regular coaching sessions, support from line managers and sponsorship from the champions will all help this group continue to grow.

     All progress needs to be reinforced. This category may turn out to be the largest group in your workforce, therefore they will need constant reassurance and confirmation about the overall direction and progress. When something isn't working out you need to make sure that this group understands what's happening. Changes in direction need to be carefully communicated so that they continue to believe that the change is worthwhile. When this group is neglected this is often the reason for a growth of discontent or negativity, or disbelief that change is really happening. Lack of motivation and the feeling of a loss of direction and momentum can easily spread.

They will also need assurance that the journey is worth making; although it may take time they will need support to make the transformation. As well as making a valuable contribution to the team or the organization, their motivation will be highest when they can see that the transformation is worthwhile for them.

3.   Discord

This is the biggest challenge to any team, organization or coach. As with group 2, a thorough assessment needs to be undertaken. Unfortunately some organizations lose good people because of mismanagement, or lack of identification of real talent. So when addressing this group the coach has a very important role to play in helping both the individual and the organization explore the reality of the discord. If we look back at the original statement, 'right people, right role, right time', with this group one or more of these will be out of step. Therefore the first assessment has to be about individuals and helping them to identify where they are in their career, what they achieved before they entered the organization, what they have achieved since entering and what they believe their potential to be.

When organizations downsize, individuals often leave without a real understanding of why they are without a job. There is often an underlying feeling of 'Why me?' As an organization transforms there may be genuine mismatches and in this context there will be occasions when an individual recognizes that his or her personal aspirations and the overall organization direction may not be aligned. There may also be a real difference between the skills and competencies of an individual and the needs and opportunities within an organization.

Unhappily too there may be a behavioural mismatch and this is often the hardest element of all. In some industries there will be managers, senior as well as junior, who were recruited and encouraged to demonstrate particular behaviours that now do not fit with the new direction of the business.

In Chapter 4 we related the responses from people about one action that organizations can take to encourage the nurturing of talent. One statement summed up the thoughts of many: 'Foster an environment in which individuals are valued and talent is exposed, nurtured and allowed to fly.' Talent management is not about a special few people. Real talent management is about playing to everyone's strengths, it is about championing diversity, encouraging creativity and innovation, but above all it is working to create an environment where the organization buzzes with energy, and people have a sparkle of anticipation when they enter their workplace.

IN SUMMARY

▌ Increasingly organizations are recognizing the importance of their intellectual property, their knowledge workers and the need to engage and retain talent. Even in the more disposable industries where employers are used to high turnover, they are beginning to recognize the cost of recruiting and training staff. As the demographics change, as talented recruits dwindle, organizations are making a more concentrated effort to retain not just talented employees.

▌ Talent is something that requires a shift in leadership thinking, a shift in the behaviour of managers and a shift in the culture and values of the business – it may also benefit from the creation of systems and processes to support the initiative – but that should not make us feel complacent that we have addressed the issue of talent if we have a talent register. That's just a fraction of the journey!

▌ Any strategy to introduce talent management must be considered in the broader context of not just attracting, retaining and motivating talent, but also addressing financial issues, such as return on investment and cost savings.

▌ Being responsible for creative and innovative ways of managing and growing own talent can be exhilarating. Individuals also need nurturing. Like plants they should be free to grow, but they need nourishment and daily watering with positive feedback if they are to thrive.

▌ Future proofing needs a holistic approach. Although there is a need to focus on retaining and developing the right people, it is also important to coordinate people development with other aspects of future proofing and this definitely means understanding what the business is trying to do.

The case study below illustrates such an approach.

TENON CASE STUDY

What does your organization do to create a culture and climate to encourage the learning potential of all employees?

We have:

▌ Underlying structure of skills and attributes to show how all can achieve potential by continual development. This emerged from basic research with the top performing staff in Tenon and so reflects what people actually need to learn to progress.

▌ Support for professional qualifications for each person if that is his or her ambition.

▌ PDRs (performance and development reviews) for all staff with a specific link with continuing professional development. Our regulatory bodies will judge individuals and Tenon by reference to this.

▌ Emphasis on development as well as performance by reviewing past performance and individual strengths to maximize future individual development.

▌ PDRs as not 'once a year' things – they are about a continuous relationship.

▌ Our intranet, TenonLink, available to all with details of all training activities. All staff are issued with booklets describing our approach and covering all jobs.

▌ Development and learning potential not just being about attending a training programme. Tenon looks at this from three angles:

– Knowing yourself – feedback, what you're good at, what you enjoy/dislike, what you find easy/hard, your values, what you want to look back on in x years' time.
– Understanding your needs – personal skills, attributes, knowledge, technical, role and responsibilities.
– Training and development – both (i) on the job: role and responsibilities, portfolio of work, opportunities in the business and (ii) off the job: training programmes, coaching/mentoring, PDR relationship, extramural roles (we have been awarded Platinum Accreditation by the ACCA for our student training programme).

How do you attract, engage and retain talented people?

I We provide a clear statement of what our aim is – to be the leading provider of business advice to owner-managed businesses and SMEs.

I We use this aim in a consistent way – through our websites, training programmes, internal communications and in external activities (Fast Track, Tenon Forum).

I All our training has been aligned with that aim under the umbrella of 'Tenon Academy'.

I Tenon Academy is a comprehensive and challenging suite of training and development activities. This includes a student programme, a personal and management development programme, an advisory programme and tailored business skills workshops. As it is a flagship training and development programme it aims to broaden the traditional role of an accountant into that of a professional business adviser.

I This sets all Tenon staff on a journey from accountant to business adviser and gives participants the confidence to tackle for clients the wide range of problems they face.

I Accountants are often categorized by specific areas of expertise. It is Tenon's firm belief that good accountants should be able to advise on a wide range of issues. Tenon Academy is helping Tenon employees better relate to their clients' wide range of concerns and is making sure that the advice they give is grounded in the reality of their client and their business.

I Tenon Academy is built around an appreciation of the personal characteristics of businessmen and women and an understanding of the key phases of business success. Whether the business is getting started, is growing out of its skin, is in a steady state, or is ready to be sold, Tenon advisers will be able to support the entrepreneur and the business through its lifecycle.

I Tenon people act as coaches on Tenon Academy programmes and build on their own skills. They also have other roles in local offices, for instance as office champions for technical training, IT projects or communications.

- We have put in place a robust promotion process, a 'Pathway to Director' aimed at promoting talent from within and establishing development plans for promising staff to help them achieve their potential.

- Our exciting and varied approach to attracting new talent is demonstrated through our innovative style of graduate recruitment literature and marketing. This is being extended to the recruitment of experienced professionals.

- We have recently introduced a company-wide 'flexible benefits' system so that people have a degree of personal choice in how they 'spend' the benefits allowance provided to them on joining.

Who drives the process and which departments were involved?

- Tenon Academy has a 100 per cent commitment from top down (CEO, operations director and finance director, operating board).

- A project team was established across line management, training and HR to make it happen.

- The whole business is involved, particularly local line management.

- We use all of the concepts in external activities – for example Fast Track – so that it aligns with our marketing effort.

How have you managed the ongoing expectations of talented people?

- Celebration of success.

- Clear and open promotion process driven by local sponsors and using a rigorous process to ensure high standards are maintained.

- Rewarding success with opportunity.

- Pay structures increasingly geared to performance with some variable reward to match individual expectations.

What are the biggest challenges in managing talent within your organization?

▮ Identifying what 'talent' looks like and interpreting that for all parts of our business.

▮ Having the right people in place identifying and managing that talent.

▮ Writing and delivering a challenging suite of training and development courses equips individuals with the tools to take back into the business to use on a day to day basis.

▮ Ongoing communication regarding who the talented people are and information to them about opportunities for development within the business.

▮ Ensuring that the way the business runs will encourage the promotion and hiring of people who will challenge us to take greater steps forward.

▮ Making sure that know-how is shared.

How have these been overcome?

▮ The creation of an environment where we applaud the ability and ambition of others.

▮ Investigation of new/innovative methods of training delivery.

▮ Management and sharing of knowledge and best practice in the business.

▮ Commitment to the best from the top down.

▮ Instilling a clear understanding that we develop people to improve on what we do, not just to achieve current standards.

▮ Informal cross-office and cross-service line groupings encouraged based on who you work with in Tenon Academy.

▮ The encouragement to allow talented people a high degree of autonomy at an early stage in their careers.

▮ Open, honest and inclusive communication through internal website, newsletters and 'all hands' days.

What have been the benefits (particularly business ones)?

We expect to see:

I decreased staff turnover and higher retention rates;

I increased staff satisfaction and morale;

I increased client satisfaction as shown in client surveys;

I tenon reputation as **the** place to be well trained to continue.

What measures or processes have you put in place to measure the effectiveness of your talent strategy?

I Monthly review at operating board of development activities.

I Relating those to measures of staff turnover and retention.

I Follow up of plans made during academy events – tracing specific plans for new business, fee growth, elimination of waste and duplication.

I Staff satisfaction surveys.

I Growth and innovation in the business – turnover and bottom line.

I Attracting talented professionals to join us.

What advice would you give to others?

I Make sure you have commitment from the top – you need solid sponsorship to be maintained (especially when budgets are being reviewed and challenges unfold as you roll a programme out into the business).

I Make sure you have the right managers in people development roles – and measure their performance in that role.

I Aim, as we do, for the creation of an environment based on inclusive relationships that celebrate all successes – your own and others.

I To do this we have to promote a clear view of our market and a sharp understanding of what our clients feel and what drives them – these elements determine their needs and how to fulfill them.

I And we do not hoard this knowledge – it is not for a select few.

About Tenon

Tenon is a leading provider of accounting and business advice to owner-managed and private businesses. Tenon provides clients with expertise in business services, tax, financial services, corporate finance, recovery, outsourcing and forensic accountancy. Tenon is a top 10 accounting firm with 1,400 staff operating through a network of 30 offices across the UK offering local expertise with the backing of a national plc.

Contact details: for further information see www.tenongroup.com

6

Talented people: what are the motivators and drivers?

Despite the best efforts of organizations to become employers of choice, build leadership teams, create new learning opportunities and seek to retain talented people, they are also fighting a battle with the talented people themselves. This is a battle that the organizations themselves cannot win, for the battle is within the individual. Maintaining interest and motivation is a daily challenge for talented people. This is particularly true of those people who rely on their creativity to succeed.

We have had years of working with talented people: people who are entrepreneurial, running their own businesses, people who feel trapped inside organizations and people who are in the fortunate position of pursuing a dream either inside or outside an organization. As part of our dialogues and surveys with these individuals we can paint a picture of some of the challenges that they face and some of the ways that line managers and organizations can support them. Within this chapter we summarize some of the comments that we have gleaned from talented people through a number of surveys over a number of years.

SO HOW DO YOU ENGAGE THE HEARTS AND MINDS OF TALENTED PEOPLE?

One place to start is in the classroom. It is well researched that many talented people actually had to overcome enormous challenges in their schooling. Business people like Richard Branson, famous sports people, artists, and many others had to overcome negative feedback from teachers or parents. Others have had to overcome personal adversity such as the loss of a parent, or other early life traumas. In *Essential Motivation in the Classroom*, Ian Gilbert (2002) describes some key strategies for motivating children and young people, but many of his suggestions are as relevant to adults as children. He describes how Japanese culture has a form of internal motivation called 'mastery'. This is the process of 'trying to be better than no one other than yourself'. He also quotes John Wooden in *Practical Modern Basketball*:

> 'True success can be attained only through self-satisfaction, in knowing you did everything within the limits of your ability to become the very best you are capable of being... Therefore, in the final analysis, only the individual himself can correctly determine his success.'

Our belief is that every individual is unique, but added to this uniqueness there are some people who are living with something else that presents them and the people or organizations with whom they interact the opportunity to really make a difference.

> 'Artists are people whose "real" job, no matter what their paying job, is the pursuit of excellence by listening carefully and well to what is trying to be born through them. Artists are not fragile, but we are delicate. We are subject to the weather conditions in our life, just as a long grey winter spent indoors can cause depression, so, too, a period where our creative life is led without the sunshine of encouragement can cause a season of despair... We cannot control everything and everybody in our creative environment... For most of us the idea that we can listen to ourselves, trust ourselves and value ourselves is a radical leap of faith. The idea that we can tell ourselves "Hey you are doing pretty well and so much better than you did last year" amounts to a revolution.'
>
> Julia Cameron, *Walking in this World* (2002)

The extract from *Walking in this World* above does not just apply to 'artists' in the purely artistic world; it also applies to the majority of human beings. We often have to work against negative feedback from others, which tells how well we are not doing, rather than how well we are doing.

'Connecting with one's dreams releases one's passion, energy and excitement about life. In leaders such passion can arouse enthusiasm in those they lead. The key is uncovering your ideal self – the person you would like to be, including what you want in your life and work... Developing that ideal image requires a reach deep inside to one's gut level.'

Daniel Goleman, _The New Leaders_ (Goleman et al, 2002)

As we have highlighted, talented people are different. They have different drivers and motivators. They are also very individual and as such there is no one universal approach that suits all talented people. Talent is not age driven; there can be a lot of emphasis on attracting young talent, but ignore experience at your peril too. The most relevant action that an organization can take is to focus on all individuals. This process should start at the recruitment stage and continue throughout the organizational lifetime of an individual, and in many cases beyond that. Real talent is in such short supply that if you identify someone who is particularly talented you may want to encourage them to return even if he or she leaves your organization to gain new experience or expertise elsewhere. Our case study companies give examples of this. Search and recruitment businesses build their reputations on keeping track of talented people; HR functions should do the same.

Consistency of approach is also important, as is honesty in performance feedback. Once you raise the expectations of talented people it is important to follow this through. There are far too many talented people who become disillusioned because their expectations were raised either during their initial interview or in ongoing appraisal discussions only to find that their manager, or the organization, reneges on commitments or promises made. Succession planning processes are a case in point. Many talented people are attracted into an organization on the promise of rapid promotion or increased responsibility, only to find that the opportunities do not really exist, or evaporate because the existing management structure holds them back.

Money or promotion are by no means the only motivators. As our research has shown, recognition, praise and feedback are equally important motivators. What talented people hate is being ignored, or, even worse, being told to stay in their box, when they have the capability to work across a number of areas.

People in traditional roles or with a more narrow perspective often fail to understand or believe the breadth of capability in a talented person, yet we have excellent examples of this in practice. One of the most famous is Leonardo da Vinci. Without doubt, da Vinci was exceptional. He not only embraced a number of artistic disciplines such as painting, drawing, sculpture, but also civil engineering, architecture, inventing and other disciplines. From his journals we also know that he applied the highest level of thought and attention to all of them.

In *How to Think Like Leonardo da Vinci* (1998), Michael Gelb describes 'Seven Da Vincian Principles that will have a real resonance with talented people.' He names the principles in Italian, and suggests that one, *'sfumato,'* is the most distinctive trait of highly creative people, a trait Leonardo probably possessed more than anyone who has ever lived. Gelb says 'as you sharpen your senses, probe the depths of experience, and awaken your childlike powers of questioning, you will encounter increasing uncertainty and ambiguity. "Confusion endurance." A willingness to embrace ambiguity, paradox and uncertainty.' We know from our research that talented people not only are comfortable in living with ambiguity, they often seek to create it.

In describing *sfumato* at work, he describes a study produced by the American Management Association, concluding that the most successful managers were distinguished by a 'high tolerance for ambiguity and intuitive decision-making skill'. Now, as the pace of change accelerates, 'tolerance' for ambiguity is no longer sufficient; ambiguity must be embraced and enjoyed. He continues by stating:

> 'In the Logic of Intuitive Decision Making, Professor Weston Agor reported his discovery, made through extensive interviews, that senior executives overwhelmingly pointed to a failure to heed their own intuition as the prime cause of their worst decisions. As we begin the twenty-first century, information threatens to overwhelm us with sheer volume. Intuition is more important than ever. The bottom line: Embrace ambiguity and trust your gut.'

Gelb presents a host of ways of stimulating an individual's creativity. Another of his principles is *curiosita*. Leonardo da Vinci carried a notebook with him at all times. He also states that, as a child, Leonardo possessed intense curiosity about the world around him.

> 'Great minds go on asking confounding questions with the same intensity throughout their ideas. Leonardo's childlike sense of wonder and insatiable curiosity, his breadth and depth of interest, and his willingness to question accepted knowledge never abated. *Curiosita* fuelled the wellspring of his genius throughout his adult life.'

Many talented people adopt such an approach, for example, Richard Branson is thought to keep a notebook; it is the only way that they are able to catch their ongoing creativity. What many of them state is surprise at how many ideas they have forgotten about when they return to the books. Da Vinci's are said to be full of drawings, notes, personal finance records, paintings, and plans for inventions. Gelb states that Bill Gates purchased eighteen sheets of Leonardo's notebooks for US $30.8 million in 1994.

As well as working with Tony Buzan and the mind-map® process, Gelb also makes reference to the work of Howard Gardner and his theory of multiple intelligences. In the context of motivating talented people, Gardner's work is presents them with a key to understanding more about how they learn and how best to learn.

Seven intelligences

In _Frames of Mind_ (1983), Howard Gardner argued that everybody possesses at least seven measurable intelligences, which he defined as follows:

1. Linguistic intelligence
   The intelligence of words. These people like to read and write, play word games, they are good at spelling, verbal and written communication. They like learning from books, tapes, lectures and presentations.

2. Logical – mathematical intelligence
   The intelligence of logic and numbers. They like experimenting with things in an orderly and controlled manner. They organize tasks into sequence. They like solving problems, they learn by creating and solving problems, playing mathematical games.

3. Musical intelligence
   The intelligence of rhythm, music and lyrics. They may play musical instruments, often sing or hum to themselves, like relaxing to music. They learn by using music, may use rhymes to help remember.

4. Spatial intelligence
   The intelligence of mental pictures and images. They think and remember in pictures, like drawing, painting, sculpting. They use symbols, doodles, diagrams and mind-maps to learn.

5. Bodily–kinaesthetic intelligence
   The intelligence of expression through physical activities. They are good with their hands, and like physical activity, sports, games, drama, dancing. They learn through doing, taking action, writing notes. They need frequent breaks when learning.

6. Interpersonal intelligence
   The intelligence of communicating with others. These are people who are good with others. They know how to organize, relate and tune into others, and put people at ease. They learn from others, like learning in teams, comparing notes, socializing and teaching.

7. Intrapersonal intelligence
   The intelligence of self-discovery. They prefer to work alone, like peace and quiet. They often daydream, are intuitive, keep a diary, plan their time carefully, and are independent. They learn by setting personal goals, taking control of their learning, reflecting on their experiences.

Gardner also added another intelligence, 'naturalistic', which is generally taken to mean the intelligence that allows individuals to relate to the natural world, to classify and to demonstrate a natural expertise in developing patterns, which can help the individual to develop order from chaos.

In Gardner's work we see how people's preferences range across more than one intelligence, and yet as we highlighted in Chapter 1, many employment tests place a higher emphasis on verbal and mathematical reasoning.

This ability to work across a number of disciplines is in direct contrast to the way many people live their lives. They have relatively simple choices, they go to school, they choose their subjects to study, they get a job, and they stay in that job or discipline. For the talented person, each day is a challenge, a new opportunity. Sometimes they drift through periods of their life, but like a dormant bulb, one day they spring awake and lurch off in new directions, convinced that it is another 'eureka' moment, and their partners and employers are caught unawares.

For talented people, their new ideas flow out of them with a passion which surprises even them. They don't quite understand the process themselves, but experience tells them to go with the flow because, just like a seam of gold, their creativity can disappear as soon as it arrives.

They have a passion to make something work, to find a new way of doing things, and often want to 'make a real difference' not just within their own working environment, but by doing something for the greater good of the organization, or humanity in general. In pursuit of this they can become completely absorbed, and can feel very frustrated when others do not have the same passions. This can be particularly true when waiting for a response or feedback from others. Because they invest so much personal energy and time in an embryonic idea, it can be very hard for them to then have to wait while their idea goes through a bureaucratic process before they get a decision about the acceptance of their idea. This often prompts creative individuals to leave an organization and to work for themselves.

One of the toughest parts of being driven by your creative thoughts is controlling this process and channelling it into a normal working environment. What do you do when you find that your mind is racing at two o'clock in the morning, particularly if it is focusing on a non-work related subject that is close to your heart and you know that the next morning you are expected to attend an internal meeting that will sap all the remaining energy that you have? All you want to do is stay with the idea that demands your attention. This is a challenge faced by all creative people. It was something that Bennis and Biedermann recognized in _Organizing Genius_ (1997). In their study of Great Groups they describe how inspiring leaders strip out the non-essentials from the lives of their creative people, saying 'Great Groups are never places where memos are the primary form of communication.'

In the US in recent times the term 'duvet day' has been coined when people ring in and say that they are spending the day in bed recovering; they are not ill but simply exhausted. This has grown up in industries where long hours have become the norm and everyone recognizes that sometimes you just have to give in to the body's need to sleep. However, many traditionalists would criticize the concept and say that it is bound to be abused. Yet in naturally creative environments, where people are genuinely involved and excited by the ideas that they are developing, when and how they work is not the issue. There are a number of examples of this way of working in our case studies.

In a work context, the application of multiple intelligences can reveal itself in individuals who can span a number of disciplines. This can present both opportunities and challenges for the individual and the organization. Given the breadth of interest in some individuals, they tend to live a dual existence. During the normal working day they apply themselves to whatever task the job requires, often shutting down parts of their mind. Outside work, a rush of creativity emerges and they have a few precious hours to indulge themselves, before sleep and the inevitability of work rolls around again.

This is highlighted by Carol Eikleberry in _The Career Guide for Creative and Unconventional People_ (1995): 'Too many artists, writers, dancers and creative people of all kinds give up the work they love in order to pay the rent. She goes on to quote Anton Chekhov, who said 'I feel more confident and more satisfied when I reflect that I have two professions and not one. Medicine is my lawful wife and literature is my mistress. When I get tired of one, I spend the night with the other. Though it is disorderly it's not so dull, and besides, neither really loses anything through my infidelity.'

Peter Cook, in *Sex, Leadership and Rock 'n' Roll* (2006), reminds us of a similar famous quote from Albert Einstein:

> 'If I were not a physicist, I would probably be a musician. I often think in music. I live my daydreams in music. I see my life in terms of music... I get most joy in life out of music.'

Few organizations can really offer the kind of flexibility that talented people need, and as mentioned above, this is why many talented people leave traditional organizations for smaller SMEs or set up their own businesses. In our work with *Mavericks* we also have countless examples of talented people who have made a choice to stay in an organization, but who know that they can give so much more. The challenge for organizations is first to recognize these individuals, and second, to use their talent in the most effective way. The model of discretionary contribution described later in this chapter is particularly relevant in finding a solution to this.

The innocent case study at the end of this chapter is an excellent example of how three entrepreneurial young men decided to set up their own business. At the very beginning they had no more than a hunch, but they were brave and they took that important first step and now they have a very successful business. Importantly in this example and other case studies, what they have done is stayed true to their values. They have grown organically by recruiting like-minded people and still maintain many of the informal, but important, small company actions as they have grown. Their company presents hope for the future. As we highlight elsewhere in this book, alignment of values with their employer is becoming increasingly important for individuals.

What is the biggest challenge about being talented?

Whilst many people would like to be talented, actually living day to day with being talented can present individuals with a number of challenges as highlighted below.

> 'Definitely putting ideas into actions. I get bored quickly and find myself wandering from the tasks at hand. No self-discipline I guess!'

> 'Too many ideas, not enough time.'

'Coming up with the initial ideas, also I find it difficult to "create" around something that I personally have little, or no interest in.'

'Never believing that I am done, or that it is good enough... Always seeing another path to go down.'

'Other people not seeing the picture, putting the details around the vision to make it happen.'

'Being creative on cue.'

'In convincing others about the utility of my ideas. Sometimes, I don't care.'

'If I am honest, I guess the most frustrating feeling is that at some time others will get the idea too even though I had it first. So I guess I like to be the first and the only, once everyone is doing it I feel disappointed and want to find something else.'

'Finding employers and colleagues who really demand and can digest creative, non-conventional. Most people seek safety and familiarity.'

'Getting others to see what's inside your head and appreciate it.'

'Being ahead of others and them not seeing the point.'

'Others who are blockers, with no/limited vision, often lazy.'

'Being prophet in my own land.'

'Maintaining the energy levels in the face of opposition.'

'Keeping to other people's pace for me; I find that many people take a lot longer to grasp concepts or pick things up than I do, so managing my own frustration can be hard. The other side is managing my impact and being aware that people can find me intimidating.'

'The hardest thing for me is being regarded as talented. Now I'm in my mid-40s I am more comfortable with this and am happier to acknowledge that I have a talent. There seems to be a "cruel" response that people have towards someone who presents themselves as talented. I don't know whether it's envy or jealousy, but I do know that life is much less painful if you hide your talent(s).'

'Self-talk, in terms of setting personal expectations, if I don't meet my own standards. I can sometimes lose balance of work/life balance because I get too focused.'

'Having to maintain your level of achievement to match both yours and other's expectations.'

'Being talented isn't a hard thing. The hard thing is utilizing that talent. As Yeats says, "the best lack all conviction, while the worst are filled with a passionate intensity."'

'Channelling one's talents into results. One may have lots of ideas and abilities, but if you can't execute them then they may as well not exist. Worse, they will fester and bubble under a frustrated surface.'

What do you enjoy most about being talented?

Being talented is not all angst. The talented people that we interviewed felt that there were some very real bonuses.

'Understanding new topics easily and being able to explain things to others in a way they can understand (my Dad says I should have been a teacher!).'

'In the same way that envious people could hurt me for expressing my talent, others nourish and uplift me when they acknowledge, value and admire what I can do.'

'Success and achievement, pushing boundaries and challenging the status quo, being able to deliver results/outcomes that people didn't think could be done, and doing it in the context of being seen to "coast along".'

'Trying new things; as a quick learner you can get on with actually doing it rather than talking about or watching others doing it.'

'I guess my skills have (so far) allowed me to live my life a certain way, and to put my writing at the centre of that. Plus, a small amount of acclaim, recognition and foreign travel.'

'Feeling tall. The centre point in a well of debate, decision, social group and general surroundings.'

'Success. Knowing that you achieved something that was better and different from conventional paths.'

'Success, the fact that you, the team or the business succeeded in doing something that others didn't, couldn't or wouldn't see.'

'Sense of achievement and the resultant exhilaration.'

'Seeing a plan come together.'

'The finished product.'

'The fun, and the difference, and the unusual, and the feeling of reward that you get... and indeed PRIDE.'

Have you ever felt 'talent capped' within an organization? What did you do as a result?

In our experience with talented people, there are times when individuals feel that their talent is not appreciated, or that the organization doesn't really know what to do with them. Unfortunately this is one of the main reasons why individuals leave organizations, as is shown in some of the comments below.

'Yes and initially I did everything I could to take more on and be given opportunities. After a period of time when it became clear that there was no scope for progression I left the organization.'

'Yes. When I started work, the organization I joined recognized people on a seniority basis rather than on talent. Later in my career I had jobs that were defined with little scope for creativity and development. I fitted in at first, later I began to push the boundaries where I could and eventually I resigned after my head began to hurt from banging up against too many brick walls.'

'Yes, left a general management/director role and started my own company.'

'Yes, a couple of times and as a result took things into my own hands and delegated tasks to free up time to do what I felt was both development for me and good for the business. Once, early in my career in HR I gave my typewriter away (along with my typing duties) to a clerk who wanted more responsibility and I got on with interviewing more new staff without ever getting authorization from my manager. I don't remember this being a big issue for anyone involved but I'm not sure I'd get away with it today!'

'Yes, where I work now. What have I done about it? Up until now, nothing. Now I am taking up a few sessions with a life coach.'

Do you ever feel that you have more talent than your organization needs? How do you channel your excess talent in work, or out of work?

We have already highlighted the very real issue of talented people often generating more ideas than they know what to deal with, and how this results in an overflow of creativity. As a result of our findings in this area we asked talented people what they did with their excess talent. As you can see from their responses, talented people are very driven and often need outlets outside of work to use up the creativity that is not used by their own organizations.

'I have felt in the past not that I had more talent than my organization needed but more than the role I was in at the time needed. It's fair to say I could apply this to my current role.'

'A channel for talent (or energy!) for me is that I consult on all the "people" aspects of business that an entrepreneurial ex-colleague of mine set up. At the same time I review all the new proposals for business ventures. Recently, I took an interior design course, bought a property and renovated it! I write. I'm currently contemplating a life coaching qualification.'

'Yes I did. This was mainly because the organization didn't know how to help people like me to recognize and utilize their talent(s) effectively.'

'While working with this organization I took every opportunity to take further study, I applied for secondments, took on additional projects and took sabbaticals to work in the voluntary sector. I also pursued my own interests outside of work developing a network and other opportunities that made better use of my talent. This supported my eventual decision to resign and set up my own company.'

'Yes, redirected my talents into studying, renovating my home, mountain bike riding, looking at other business ventures. Also did a lot of work with industry associations.'

'As someone who is now running their own training consultancy, I can pretty much do as I want and therefore do spend my time doing more of what I want to do rather than what I don't. I also plan time in my week to pursue other interests where I can utilize other passions/ talents.'

'Yes. Other than get frustrated, I run, rant and ridicule.'

Can you describe a perfect scenario when you really felt in tune with your talent, or in your ideal world how would you make best use of your talent?

Helping talented people recognize the best way of making use of their talent is an important part of motivating talented people. Unfortunately, many people get frustrated because they cannot maximize their talent in their current organizations. The exceptions are those people who have taken control of their destiny and are working for themselves.

'I have yet to realize what my talents are. I believe that they might be humour, communication and organization. Once I understand and respect my own abilities, then I can move forward.'

'In an ideal world I would be running a business with like-minded individuals or working for myself in a consultative role.'

'I am often in tune with my talent these days. Running my own work and life balance company puts my talent and the talents of those that work with me to best use. When we deliver an inspiring workshop, or do a great piece of one-to-one behavioural change work with someone. When we coach a team or individual to develop their own talent(s) or go on to achieve their goals, it develops that feeling of self-worth and purpose. It allows us to put our talents to best use for greater good in the world.'

'When I got my 15 minutes of fame, and my Disney conference was an obvious success and attention to detail, creativity, leadership, planning and organization all coming to the fore at the right place and at the right pace. Maslow was right. Self-actualization!'

'When someone really, really trusts that you can do it.'

'My current situation; I am leading and building my company, focusing on those areas where I think organizations are lacking. People pay and actively seek my advice as an expert, I get to tangibly measure success by the success of the intervention, the rewards are high and the risks are high; this adds brevity to the situation, which in turn means that I feel that I am doing something that is worthwhile.'

'This is difficult, looking back it's hard to remember any conscious thinking or actions at times when I have felt successful. It's only as one looks back at a situation that one can see, often with surprise, that "it's worked!"'

'I'm hopefully moving towards that. I think the perfect scenario would be where I could find the people who were most appreciative of my talent.'

HOW CAN HR HELP TO MOTIVATE TALENTED PEOPLE?

As we highlight in Chapters 2 and 9, HR can sometimes feel under enormous pressure and, as a result, taking time out to consider your own motivators and drivers can be at the bottom of a very long list of actions. However, considering your own role, what you have achieved and your plans for the future can be a very important part of your own development. HR and learning and development personnel are often so busy with responding to the needs of the rest of the business that they forget to consider themselves. HR directors can also be guilty of ignoring either their own development, or the development of their own team.

What about the brand of the HR department? What messages does your department give to the rest of the business? Have you created an environment which is energetic, ideas-driven and a centre of excellence? Or is it business-like and purposeful, weighed down by the responsibility of everyday dealings of pay and rations? It is possible to be responsible and imaginative, creative and exciting. What it takes is careful planning, resource management and inspiring leadership.

If you want to motivate others it is important to consider how you motivate yourself. One way of doing this is to undertake a self-motivation audit. This list below is created in the context of wanting to achieve a particular ambition. As a starting point you may want to identify something that you would really like to achieve, either in or out of work. One thing you might want to focus on is how to raise the profile of both yourself and the department. Here are some questions that you may want to ask yourself:

1.   What do I really know about me?
     How you describe yourself to others is only the very top layer; underneath is a whole cocktail of hopes and fears, attitudes and behaviours. When you apply for a job you are often asked to complete a variety of tests, which may give you information about your personality traits, your skills and aptitude. The more you know about you, the more you understand about how you will respond in certain situations. If you have been in the same role for a while, why not update your knowledge of yourself by undertaking either psychometric tests or a personal preference inventory? (The authors have developed a number of inventories: see Chapter 10 for contact details.) Take every opportunity presented to you to build up your picture of yourself.

2.   What do I do really well?
     One of the failings in society at large is to give people enough positive feedback about what they have done well. We rarely thank people individually when they have done something for us. Equally, individuals often do not know how to respond when they are thanked, or given a compliment; there is a lot of looking down and shuffling. Knowing what you do well and taking time to thank others is an important part of building confidence. Making a list of your strengths is an important first step in achieving an ambition. Think about the checklist in Chapter 2, which highlighted the qualities below:

     – a belief in one's own ability;
     – personal presence;
     – wisdom, knowledge, or particular expertise;
     – ability to persuade others;

    – status that is respected by others;
    – a special something that makes others want to believe in someone, be with them, or follow them.

Which of the above do you and your team have? Which ones do you want? Which could you develop?

3.   What would I like to do better?
One of the most important factors in becoming more self-aware is really working to understand yourself and focusing on self-development. Self-confidence is developed over time from a heightened awareness of your own abilities and competence through handling real issues and challenges. By looking for opportunities continually to build your knowledge and broaden your experience, you will be building a solid foundation from which all development can grow. Take time to explore opinions, ask open questions, and seek clarification. As well as knowing your strengths it is also important to recognize areas that you need to work on. By identifying them for yourself you can take responsibility for improving them. We all have things that we would like to improve, but there may also be areas where you say 'Actually, I don't think I will ever be able to do that well. If it is important to my job who do I know who I could work in partnership with?'

4.   How do I react under pressure?
There is a maturity of approach, which only comes by self-discovery. There is a big difference between handling stress and pressure. People can respond positively and actually withstand a certain amount of pressure, but the physical impact of stress can be quite different. You need to ask yourself what puts you under pressure and then find ways of coping with it. Getting yourself in shape physically and mentally can be an important part of your preparation.

    Think about the ways you handle challenging situations. Do you prepare effectively for them? Do you assess your own capabilities? Do you contact colleagues and other team members who have relevant expertise? Are you willing to ask for help?

5.   What will prompt me into taking action?
As mentioned previously at the beginning of this chapter, one of the biggest reasons why people do not achieve their ambitions is apathy; there is always a reason not to get started, to get deflected from your goals, to give up when it gets difficult. By understanding how to motivate yourself, how to make your ambition more

achievable, it suddenly becomes much easier to get started and to keep going. As well as being able to motivate others it is important to be able to motivate yourself. One of the profiles that we have developed is 'Motivation to Change', which identifies your preferences in handling change (see Chapter 10 for Kaye Thorne's contact details).

6.   Who do I trust to give me feedback?
One way that we really change our behaviour is through feedback from others. How open are you to feedback? Do you actively seek the opinion of others who may have a different viewpoint? Do you ask for clarification? Are you able to integrate these views with the views of others and your perception of yourself? We all need feedback – it helps us to grow and develop and to gain a greater understanding of our strengths and development areas – but we also need to find the right people to give it to us. Unfortunately, too few people are really skilled at giving it. Try and find people whose opinion you trust and value and ask them to help you understand yourself better. Do you understand how your emotions affect your behaviour, and the impact on others?

7.   What is really important in my life?
How prepared are you to accept the need to change? Once you have received feedback, how proactive are you in doing things differently? How willing are you to absorb the feedback and develop new ways of behaving? Before starting on the journey to achieve your ambition it is often helpful to take stock and identify what is important to you; particularly if your ambitions are particularly challenging, or will involve you in making personal sacrifices. You need to anchor what you want to nurture and cherish and what is less important. Physically clearing out the clutter that surrounds you is another way of getting ready.

8.   Who could really inspire me to achieve my ambition?
There may be one or two people who you know have that special ability to inspire you and to help you through the hard times. Treasure them and value what they can offer you and also see if you can inspire them too. Finding a soul mate is a very special feeling; never take the relationship for granted. Are you someone that others turn to? Do you inspire trust? Do you help others through the tough times? Giving an impression of quiet confidence can inspire others to support you and help the team pull together. What could you do to be more consistent in your

support? Do you have a network of people who can stimulate, energize and support you? How active is your network, how often do you review your contacts? Identify any gaps or opportunities for extending your network; include people in and outside of work. When was the last time you did something for someone in your network? Proactively seek to help others.

Self-motivation is not easy. If it was there would be no challenge, no excitement, and no sense of achievement when you finally reach your goal. However, if you understand the challenges you will be better able to motivate others.

DISCRETIONARY CONTRIBUTION

In terms of motivating talented people, you first have to understand them. In reading the comments from talented people in this chapter we hope that you now have a greater insight into what motivates and drives them. One of their biggest challenges is trying to manage their creativity, both in terms of when it happens, but also in terms of the sheer volume of ideas, passions and genuine enthusiasm. Helping them to identify which ideas are worth pursuing, finding other ways of progressing ideas that they have lost interest in, and helping them integrate with others are some of the ways that you can help them fulfil their potential both as individuals and also as major contributors to the success of the business. What is equally important is recognizing the importance of not just talented people, but all employees and what they choose to contribute. If we look at the model below it illustrates the key stages and in many ways is similar to Maslow's theory of motivation and his 'Hierarchy of Needs'.

1. Willingness to attend
   This first stage is based on an assumption that individuals, once recruited, are willing to attend your organization. At this stage their drivers may very much be based on the sentiment 'It's a job.' They will have very little loyalty and may not yet feel very engaged with the organization.

2. Willingness to contribute
   At this stage the individual, as well as entering through the gates of your organization, are willing to make a contribution. How they continue to make that contribution will very much depend on the

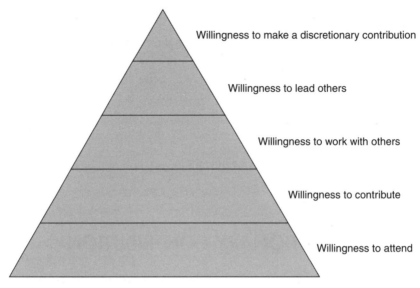

Willingness to make a discretionary contribution

Willingness to lead others

Willingness to work with others

Willingness to contribute

Willingness to attend

Source: The Inspiration Network

Figure 6.1 Model of discretionary contribution

expectations of their performance, how successful they feel they are and the feedback that they receive.

3. Willingness to work with others
   Assuming that they are successful and the encouragement they receive and the impact of other team members on them, they start interacting, one hopes positively with others.

4. Willingness to lead others
   Over a period of time they may demonstrate leadership qualities, which provide them with an opportunity to progress. This may mean more money, but it may also mean leaving familiar work and teammates behind. Some choose this route, others refuse this opportunity. Talented people sometimes do not want responsibility for others. The more creative and 'maverick' individuals rarely want to manage others; they find it hard enough managing themselves.

5. Willingness to make a discretionary contribution
   At this stage individuals go beyond their required contribution to offer a discretionary contribution. The assumption is that people

in this zone recognize the contribution that they make in their normal day to day work, but they also choose to offer more than is required. This may include volunteering, working extra time on a project, thinking about ideas outside of work, willingness to represent the company externally. Above all it is an attitude of mind, which engages with the heart and soul, which encourages an employee to go the extra mile for an organization. Many SMEs' successes are built on discretionary activity, because the individual feels their values are aligned with the organization and together they are pursuing a common goal.

Finally, here is checklist of actions for HR or line managers to help motivate talented people:

I Recognize that one size does not fit all in terms of personal development; be genuinely interested in all individuals, but be aware that talented people may have different needs, so ask them about their hopes and aspirations. Encourage them to identify what they feel they need in terms of development.

I Motivate people by tapping into their values and passions. Enthuse people with your own energy. Spend time with them. Show genuine interest in them and their lives outside work.

I People have a range of needs, including physical, financial, social and psychological needs. Individuals need to find the work itself both challenging and rewarding. They need you give them positive feedback when they do well. Remember that good motivators lead by example.

I Delegate real authority to people, giving them the power to make decisions, and the support and the information that they need to do this. Give people recognition, show you value them, and encourage them to take responsibility. Monitor and give them constructive feedback on their performance.

Ask yourself:

I What do I know about me that would help me motivate others?

I How inspiring am I?

I Do I appear genuinely interested in others?

I How effective are my relationships with others?

I How do I deal with people who are difficult to motivate?

I What different strategies could I adopt that would help me motivate more effectively?

I How enthusiastic am I about wanting to motivate myself?

I What could I learn from others?

I Who could I ask to give me really useful feedback?

To return to Cameron's *Walking in this World* (2002):

'We all know people who tell us our dreams are foolish, pie in the sky whimsy and that we should be grateful for what recognition we have won and settle for a lower creative ceiling than our high-flying dreams require. (Those people have settled themselves and are uncomfortable with anyone willing to continue with substantial risks.) Fortunately, we also know people who do not bother to think about the odds, or age, or anything but the work at hand. Those people are the ones we must consciously choose to listen to... If we are to "take heart" and go on with our work, then we must take our heart seriously. We must listen to its pains and we must bring to it, its joys. A heart does not need to be told, "Oh, toughen up." It needs you to plan a tiny cheering ceremony and execute it. That done you will find "the heart" – the courage – to work again and well.'

IN SUMMARY

I Our belief is that every individual is unique, but added to this uniqueness there are some people who are living with something else that presents them, and the people or organizations with whom they interact, the opportunity really to make a difference.

I Above all it is an attitude of mind, which engages with the heart and soul, which encourages an employee to go the extra mile for an organization. Many SMEs' successes are built on discretionary activity, because the individual feels their values are aligned with the organization and together they are pursuing a common goal.

I As we have highlighted, talented people are different. They have different drivers and motivators. They are also very individual and as such there is no one universal approach that suits all talented people. The most relevant action that an organization can take is to focus on all individuals. This process should start at the recruitment stage and continue throughout the organizational lifetime of an individual, and in many cases beyond that.

❙ Helping talented people to identify which ideas are worth pursuing, finding other ways of progressing ideas that they have lost interest in, and helping them integrate with others are some of the ways that you can help them fulfil their potential both as individuals and also as major contributors to the success of the business. What is equally important is recognizing the importance of not just talented people, but all employees and what they choose to contribute.

❙ Real talent is in such short supply that if you identify someone who is particularly talented you may want to encourage them to return even if they leave your organization to gain new experience or expertise elsewhere.

The case study below is an excellent example of how to motivate talented employees.

INNOCENT CASE STUDY

Innocent is one of the best examples of how to grow talent, naturally and organically. The story of its start up is legendary: the company was founded by Adam Balon, Jon Wright and Richard Reed, three young friends from college who wanted to set up a business together.

In the summer of 1998, they bought £500 worth of fruit, turned it into smoothies and took them to a jazz festival to try out their idea. They put up a big sign saying 'Do you think we should give up our jobs to make these smoothies?' and put out a bin saying 'YES' and a bin saying 'NO', asking people to try one of their drinks and then to put their empty bottle in the appropriate bin. At the end of the weekend, the 'YES' bin was full so they went to work the next day and resigned. Things have been going from strength to strength since that day. And it seems that Rich, Adam and Jon's belief that people really do want to buy great tasting and totally natural drinks to help them stay healthy, and that they don't mind paying a bit extra to get them, was right.

Since 1999, innocent has extended its range of drinks to nine smoothies, two of which change each season, two of which are super smoothies (each ingredient chosen for its particular benefit) and one of which is fruit and vegetable. Four of the smoothie recipes are available in one-litre take home cartons as well as 250ml bottles. There is also a thickie (yoghurt based fruit drink), four juicy waters and a fresh orange juice. The company has even published a smoothie recipe book called *Little Book of Drinks* and a simple guide to being healthy called 'Stay Healthy, Be Lazy'. The team has expanded from just 3 people to almost 90, all based at Fruit Towers in West London.

innocent drinks are available in over 4,000 outlets, from independents like cafes and health food stores to multiples like Waitrose and Sainsbury's all over the UK, Ireland and increasingly Europe too (Holland, France and Belgium).

The company has grown from having zero to over 50 per cent market share, last year the turnover was £16.7 million and this year it is aiming for over £35 million. It is now the number one smoothie brand in the UK.

From the start there was an energy and enthusiasm. Everyone was involved in everything; some might call it multitasking, but in the day to day working of the company it was just the most natural thing to do. People helped where they were needed most. In terms of recruitment, friends joined and then friends of friends. People who had been travelling came and brought new skills or developed skills on the job.

From the very beginning, one of its key strategies has been 'Happy People'. This applies in all aspects of its business from employees to customers to anyone who comes in contact with their company. The three founder members enjoyed spending time with each other and they wanted to create an environment where everyone would enjoy coming to work. Yet behind this apparent informality there were also some very sound principles of people development. All employees have a job description, every week they have an informal chat with their manager, every six months they have a more formal 360 degree assessment, which includes the individual's personal criteria, together with the company criteria. In this way everyone has an understanding of how they can contribute to the company's overall objectives and the company knows how it can support individuals. Every week there is a Monday morning meeting that everyone attends from the whole company and there is an update of the critical issues for the week. As the company grows it takes longer to run the meeting, but everyone sees it as a really helpful way of keeping up to date. Once a quarter there is a bigger overview, and everyone in the company is aware of the overall vision, the plans for the year and the next five years.

When new people join innocent they know they are joining something different. Although they are given a job description, they get to choose the title that is in keeping with the overall innocent style, eg one of the PR people is called 'Juice Press', the HR person is called 'People Person', and all of the founders are called 'Chief Squeezers'. On their first day new people are given a guide to the company ethos and the culture, and also a timetable of people who are to be their 'lunch mates' for the first two weeks, which gives people new to the organization the opportunity to meet at least 10 people who they can question informally to help induct them into the company. Other people will also make sure that they take time informally to say hello and welcome the new people into the company.

Every Friday they have 'Friday Beers' at Fruit Towers or a local pub, where for a few hours the whole company takes time out and relaxes together. Every year there is a tradition of taking some kind of annual nature break together, because the three founder members came up with the idea on holiday. They celebrate once a year, and this year the 65 members of the company went to Switzerland for a weekend snowboarding break.

Informally, everyone at innocent has become an ambassador for the company. When they socialize with their friends they often share their enthusiasm about the company, and others have joined as a result of hearing about the style and culture of the company.

innocent is equally committed to 'giving something back' and takes its social and corporate responsibility very seriously. From the very beginning, because its products are so fresh, it has always given any surplus to the charity Fair Share to give to the homeless. In 2005, to say thank you to all its drinkers innocent held a two-day free music festival in Regent's Park, 'Fruitstock', and invited all its outlets, journalists and other contacts to a special enclosure called 'Very Nice People', which was an opportunity to get to know people in an informal and special way. It also gave the opportunity for 120,000 of the general public to find out more about innocent and to enjoy the event. The year 2005 was the third year for Fruitstock and innocent is planning to continue the tradition. innocent has also set up the registered charity 'innocent foundation' with an aim of helping other charities that have a commitment to bringing nature and community closer together both in the UK and globally. The innocent foundation is funded completely by profits from innocent's main company and staffed by innocent people.

With so much that works at innocent there has to be the question 'What are the challenges?' One challenge has been finding the right people soon enough. Growing organically has sometimes meant that individuals have had to wait longer than perhaps the company wanted to find the right people to support them. Predicting the rate of growth is always a challenge, but innocent is well on the way to meeting its mission: 'To become Europe's favourite little juice company'.

innocent has also won many awards and accolades, including:

I Young Entrepreneurs of the Year at the Ernst & Young Entrepreneur Awards 2003;

I Small to Medium Sized Business of the Year award at the National Business Awards 2002;

I Best Customer Service award at the Growing Business Awards 2003;

I Marketing Campaign of the Year for small to medium sized business at the Marketing Society Awards 2003 and at the National Business Awards 2003;

I Best Use of Innovation at the Orange Small is Beautiful Awards 2003;

I Best UK Soft Drink both 2002 and 2003 at the Quality Food & Drink Awards;

I gold medals at the Great Taste Awards for four years in a row;

I came out top in the Top 100 UK Employers 2005 (*Guardian*)

I National Business Awards 2004 – winner in the Employer of the Year award;

I National Business Awards 2003 – finalist in the Outstanding People Development award;

I National Business Awards 2002 – winners of the People Development award.

Contact details: e-mail Bronte@innocentdrinks.co.uk

7

How to create the right environment for talent to thrive

Successfully working with talented people means engaging with them and recognizing where they are on their development path. For some it could have been a rocky journey; we have already mentioned some of the very real challenges faced by talented people. They may have started off in school as naturally curious, energetic and full of enthusiasm, only to find that peer pressure or poor teaching may have dimmed some of their hopefulness. In developing talent, what you are seeking to do is to push the right buttons to help them connect with their latent talent again. Depending where they are in their development path you may also be faced with highly energized, motivated and challenging talented people, or older, more maverick individuals, who have seen most of it before and who do not suffer fools easily.

Against this backdrop, it is little wonder than organizations do not necessarily know how to handle talent. One way of starting is to gather as much knowledge as possible about how people learn and match this to the needs of the talented people that you are working with.

WHAT DO WE KNOW ABOUT TALENTED PEOPLE?

Talented people:

I may have limited attention span;

I curious;

I set themselves ambitious goals;

I easily bored;

I don't suffer fools;

I many plates in the air;

I generate more ideas than they can ever implement;

I work long and hard when interested;

I want to be somewhere else when bored.

WHAT DO THEY WANT?

Talented people want:

I recognition;

I feeling of achieving something significant;

I excitement;

I variety;

I stimulation;

I feeling of making a difference.

WHAT CONDITIONS DO TALENTED PEOPLE THRIVE IN?

Talented people are often complex, and do not necessarily understand themselves what they want, as they are in a continual process of growth.

As some of our earlier feedback has revealed sometimes they drive and drive to get something, only to find when they finally get it they have lost interest in it. One major factor is boredom, and the need for new challenges. Talented people themselves, when they do understand what they need, try to create environments that work for them.

As we highlighted in Chapter 1, they probably work harder than others at creating a more effective work/life balance because it is important to them. However, when they are motivated and interested in something they also will drive themselves to incredible lengths. Also, talented people can often can only respond when they are up against a deadline. Time and time again we hear the same response from talented people when they recognize that no matter how early they receive a deadline, it is only when the final pressure is on that they respond. While this often provides them with an adrenaline rush to complete the task, this is often a pattern that is repeated and can cause immense frustration for other people who are waiting for their response.

Talented people vary in their requirements for other people: some need others as a sounding board, or just to be around to talk to, socialize with, or to be there to welcome them back from their thinking time. Others prefer to be more solitary, particularly if they are trying to be creative.

'I am most innovative when I am travelling in the car, walking in the countryside, in the bath, just before bed/first thing in the morning, usually those times when we sort of half switch off. I am also very creative when I can bounce off others who are inspirational and innovative too. At those times the environment isn't that important because we sort of get caught up in the ideas and don't notice.'

'Spacious, relaxed, light, quiet environment, preferably discussing with other people, with lots of paper and pens.'

'Quiet, thoughtful time, sometimes some calming or thought provoking music.'

'Relaxing, drinking with friends.'

'Working with a team of friends to try to achieve difficult tasks.'

'The friend thing is important – a comfortable environment is important as is the feeling that my observations will be valued no matter how outlandish.'

'Freedom to explore new ideas, with others happy to contribute and add value. Requires trust and some basic processes to support.'

'Usually under pressure when the standard or obvious solutions won't work. I usually find that desperation is the mother of invention.'

'Pressure/short deadlines/urgent problems/problems that someone else can't solve.'

'I like lots of quiet reflective time on my own, maybe with music and nature around, but I also know that I get sparks from contact with other people, from energy and noise, and from being forced to deliver within constraints. The key word is flexibility – the ability to move from one set of conditions to another as necessary or as the mood, context, people and process take me.'

'It obviously also depends on:

▌ [whether] this a solo piece of creativity or a team effort – what helps me be creative on my own (quiet, music etc) is not necessarily what will help to shift a stuck group;

▌ the purpose – creative could mean high art, or craft, or thinking about how to design a product;

▌ if it is something I have done before (leave me to it) or something brand new (let me reflect but give me information and prompts too);

▌ if we are taking an exploratory step in the process, or a focusing step – different thinking styles and different conditions help.'

'Peace and quiet – no distractions. I also like to walk round a room when thinking. However, many ideas come when outside of work, out running, in the bath, etc.'

'Creativity is not limited to nine to five. A variety of conditions: it could vary from being under pressure to after lunch, dozing; it's in that half-conscious connection with a near dreamlike state that ideas can flow. Walking also helps.'

'Usually at my best on a one-to-one with another who is receptive to and wants to co-create. Freewheeling, letting the thought processes take me.'

'Being faced with problems whilst working in a situation where I am able to discuss them with supportive colleagues, who I trust, and then having freedom to act. Enjoying what I'm doing and having fun doing it.'

'Natural light, barefoot, somewhere relaxed. Bursts of no more than one hour.'

'Relaxation, freedom from stress and time pressure, support of colleagues. But after the creating phase I don't mind a deadline for the realization/report phase.'

HOW DO TALENTED PEOPLE PREFER TO LEARN?

As a group, talented people probably gain most pleasure from learning, and are likely to see it as a lifelong process. One of the comments from one of our respondents was as follows:

> 'Viewing self as a product that has to be totally reinvented every three to four years.'

This statement is a very accurate assessment of the process that talented people either consciously or unconsciously undergo throughout their lives. Others may marvel at the way that talented people seem to pick themselves up after a setback, or keep going on new projects long after they have made significant sums of money, or past retirement age.

Many people prefer to learn through doing or, as Kolb might describe it, 'active experimentation' (see below). Other learners prefer conversations with others as a sounding board, or with someone who is like-minded, who can help them explore their ideas further, adding to their picture, or reshaping certain aspects of it. This also reflects the way that many people prefer to learn, discovering with others rather than being told the facts by a specialist. What is important is the need for feedback. Even though individuals may want to learn through discovery, they also want to know how well they are doing and to have access to coaching when they need it.

How we learn is one of the most individual and personal activities that we ever undertake and yet most of us spend most of our learning lumped together in learning environments which give us very little opportunity for individual coaching and support. For creative and innovative people, whatever their age, this is even harder. They crave feedback, they need time to reflect, they want very specific coaching to help them develop what they know they need to know. Unlike many others, they often have a purpose to their learning and they get incredibly frustrated with what they may perceive as trivia, or irrelevant information.

We know through the work of Paul Torrance, David Kolb, Honey and Mumford, Daniel Goleman and Howard Gardner (see Chapter 6) that people respond positively to different learning stimuli, and yet many corporate environments strip out the senses. There is still so much work to do to help organizations, whether they are schools, further or higher education institutes or places of employment, become somewhere where individuals enthusiastically want to attend. Below is a summary of some of the key theories behind how people learn. It is very likely that you will already be familiar with a number of them, and if so we apologize for including them again. However, what is important is that many people in organizations are less familiar with them and taken together they provide a very useful blueprint for engaging with talented learners.

MAKING LEARNING A REAL EXPERIENCE

'The hidden message from my school, I eventually realized, was not only crippling it was wrong. The world is not an unsolved puzzle, waiting for the occasional genius to unlock its secrets. The world, or most of it, is an empty space waiting to be filled. That realization changed my life. I did not have to wait and watch for the puzzles to be solved, I could jump into the space myself. I was free to try out my ideas, invent my own scenarios, create my own futures.'

Charles Handy, *Beyond Certainty*

Many adults equate learning with experiences that they would rather forget, so awakening the learning giant within is a real challenge, but also a fantastic opportunity. There is a lot of focus on the phrase 'lifelong learning', but to achieve it takes far more than the setting up of government initiatives. It means enabling people to understand, explore and then take ownership of the learning that really matters for them. The very nature of this approach has to mean that the 'one size fits all' approach really doesn't work, just like the misshapen T-shirt with the label 'one-size' it cannot compare to the unique tailoring and fit of a made to measure garment. Learning that means something important, personal and special to the individual will have far more impact than a generic learning product. So how can we apply this principle to working with talented people?

One of the most enduring models about learning is Kolb's learning cycle; he identified the key steps in how people learn. He defined those steps as follows:

Having an experience

Whether it is managing a project, giving a presentation, or completing a development activity. Searching out new and challenging experiences, problems and opportunities. Finding like-minded people to learn with. Making mistakes and having fun.

Reviewing the experience...

...and reflecting on what went well and what could have been improved, as well as seeking feedback from others. Standing back from events to watch, listen and think. Listening to a wide cross-section of people with varying views. Investigating by probing, assembling and analysing information. Reviewing what has happened, and what you have learned.

Theorizing about what happened and why, then exploring options and alternatives

Questioning and probing logic and assumptions. Exploring ideas, concepts, theories, systems and models. Exploring interrelationships between ideas, events and situations. Formulating your own theories or models.

Planning what to do differently next time

Finding out how the experts do it. Looking for practical applications of ideas. Finding opportunities to implement or teach what you learn. Trying out and practising techniques with coaching and feedback.

It is important to recognize that not all learning may take place in a neat and ordered way. We learn best when we combine all four approaches to learning:

▌ theory input;

▌ practical experience;

▌ application of theory;

▌ idea generation.

Kolb's learning cycle is also linked to the work of Honey and Mumford and their Learning Styles Questionnaire. We all prefer to learn in slightly different ways:

▌ activists learn best by doing;

▌ reflectors learn best by observing;

▌ theorists learn best by thinking things through in a logical and systematic manner;

▌ pragmatists like to learn through putting their ideas into practice and testing them out.

To find out more detail about you or your learner's preferred learning style you may wish to undertake the Honey and Mumford Learning Styles Questionnaire (www.peterhoney.com). The definitions below give you some examples of the different types of learning style. Try to identify which of the learning styles appeals to you or the person with whom you are working.

Activists

I enjoy new experiences and opportunities from which they can learn;

I often do things first and think about it later;

I enjoy being involved, are happy to be in the limelight and prefer to be active rather than sitting and listening;

I often look for new challenges;

I like to learn with people who are like-minded;

I are willing to make mistakes;

I like to have fun when they are learning.

Reflectors

I prefer to stand back from events, to watch and absorb information before starting;

I like to hear other people's viewpoint;

I like to review what has happened, and what they have learned;

I prefer to reach decisions in their own time;

I do not like to feel under pressure.

Theorists

I like to explore methodically to think problems through in a step-by-step logical way and ask questions;

I can be detached and analytical;

I like to be intellectually stretched and may feel uncomfortable with lateral thinking, preferring models and systems;

I prefer to come up with their own theories or models.

Pragmatists

▌ like practical solutions and want to get on and try things;

▌ dislike too much theory;

▌ sometimes like to find out how the experts do it;

▌ like to experiment and search out new ideas that they want to try out;

▌ tend to act quickly and confidently;

▌ very down to earth and respond to problems as a challenge.

You may find that you have a preference for one or two learning styles, or you may find that like a small percentage of people, you have a balanced learning style. Kolb's ideas about learning and Honey and Mumford's learning styles link well together. They link with the following model of how people learn something new:

Unconscious incompetence

I don't know what I don't know and I don't know that I don't know it. Ignorance is bliss!

Conscious incompetence

I know there are things that I should know, but I am not able to do them yet.

Conscious competence

I know what I should know, and how to use my knowledge to put it effectively into practice.

Unconscious competence

I now do things without consciously thinking about how I do it.

Using the whole brain

As well as understanding your learning style you will also have a preferred way of operating through your left, or right brain. The research of Sperry and Onstein showed that we have two hemispheres in our brain, which have different characteristics or functions.

LEFT BRAIN	RIGHT BRAIN
Logic	Rhythm
List	Colour
Linear	Imagination
Words	Day dreaming
Numbers	Intuition
Sequence	Spatial awareness
Analysis	Music

If you have always primarily used one side of your brain you may find it harder to use the other. You may believe that you are no good at a particular subject, eg you may say 'I am no good at maths,' or 'I've never been able to draw'. However, researchers like Tony Buzan (Buzan@mind-map.com) who developed the mind-maps® technique are showing that we need not be dominated by either the left or the right brain, but that by using both sides of our brain in our activities become more 'whole-brained'.

Mind-mapping® is a powerful way of expressing thoughts. The basic technique is to combine lines, text and images to represent related ideas and concepts. The technique can be used in a variety of contexts including note taking, summaries of visits, sales calls, problem solving, decision-making, planning and designing training, life planning and career choices, etc. Buzan emphasizes the importance of seeing mind-maps® as a whole-brain activity. One of the great advantages of mind-maps® is that large amounts of information can be summarized on one page, and from the initial map project plans can be created. Further information is available through www.buzanworld.com.

Another technique is de Bono's 'Six Thinking Hats'. With Six Thinking Hats, Edward de Bono shows how to maximize your own mind's effectiveness and help groups work creatively together. He uses a technique to separate thinking into different types. For further information see www.Edwdebono.com.

Once you understand your preferences, and the more you understand about how you learn, you can use this knowledge to accelerate your learning and to make your learning experiences more meaningful.

We have already mentioned the work of Howard Gardner and his theory of multiple intelligences in Chapter 6. Howard's work is also linked to the work of Daniel Goleman and emotional intelligence.

Emotional intelligence

Increasingly both individuals and organizations are also recognizing the richness that can be considered by examining areas that are more personal, such as the Emotional Competence framework as identified by Daniel Goleman in his book *Working with Emotional Intelligence* (1998).

Although it may seem that the phrase 'emotional intelligence' is a recent entrant into our vocabulary, it has in fact been acknowledged for a much longer period. Goleman suggests that a number of people have defined emotional intelligence, including Howard Gardner who in 1983 proposed the model of 'multiple intelligence'. Peter Salovey and John Mayer (1997) defined emotional intelligence 'in terms of being able to monitor and regulate one's own and others' feelings and to use feelings to guide thought and action.'

Goleman's own definition includes 'five basic emotional and social competencies':

▌ self-awareness;

▌ self-regulation;

▌ motivation;

▌ empathy;

▌ social skills.

Goleman's work moves emotional intelligence into the arena of emotional competence, by further defining 25 emotional competencies and explaining that individuals will have a profile of strengths and limits, but that 'the ingredients for outstanding performance require only that we have strengths in a given number of these competencies typically at least six or so and that the strengths be spread across all five areas of emotional intelligence. In other words there are many paths to excellence.'

What Goleman and others have done is to introduce the concept of another type of intelligence and suggest that our skills with people are as important to the organizations that might recruit us as our IQ, our qualifications and our expertise.

Many organizations are also recognizing the impact of this in their retention and development of key workers. These personal competencies together with other traits and characteristics present vital clues to creating meaningful learning experiences.

If the talented people you are working with enjoy the learning experience, they are more likely to learn and remember. If they are told they need to learn something, their willingness to learn will depend on the respect that they have for the person telling them and their desire to learn. If their desire to learn is driven by a personal curiosity and they learn in a way that reflects their preferred learning style, it is likely that their own enthusiasm and interest will make the learning more meaningful and memorable. In order to create meaningful learning experiences, teachers, lecturers, trainers and workplace coaches and individual learners could do so much more to develop effective learning patterns.

Ironically, much pre-school and early years learning does focus on more stimulating ways of learning. Unfortunately, many of the opportunities really to experience learning seem to disappear as individuals progress through school and career.

If we are focusing on how to create an environment where talent can thrive, another important area is talent and the management structure.

HOW DO TALENTED PEOPLE LIKE TO BE MANAGED?

This is a major question for both talented people and the management hierarchy within organizations. As we have shown earlier, organizations want to recruit talented people. In many organizations talent equates to future leaders and in this context talented people are groomed, developed and supported as they progress through an organization. They are mentored, coached and encouraged to develop leadership skills and competencies.

However, other talented people are recruited for their ideas and creativity because the organization wants to increase its innovation. These talented people may have very little interest in managing anyone else, in many ways prefer to work by themselves, and do not necessarily respond to being managed. In our research we found evidence of both mindsets.

'I don't respond well to being overseen.'

'I need a lot of freedom, but staging posts/deadlines are essential.'

'Full responsibility, but sometimes, purely as a change it is nice to receive direction and be absolved of responsibility, not for long though.'

'Delegation is very important. Once the concept is fully formed I want to inspire others to help bring it to fruition.'

'Yes, quite enjoy coaching people in my team and bringing them on.'

'Guide not controller – only like working with self-motivated people.'

'Depends – if it is coordinating other self-motivated people that's OK; not if it's telling people what to do.'

There was also a desire for other people to also take responsibility for themselves, ie talented people do not mind leading or guiding people, but they do not want to micro-manage:

'Yes, for those who don't need to have their hand held.'

'It's a necessary part of my job but I would prefer that my team took a high level of responsibility for themselves (and am encouraging them to do so).'

Some respondents also saw it as a more long-term opportunity; others made the link between the way that they were managed and the way they wanted to manage others:

'I liked managing others because of the clear development of people's talents, confidence and skills in the environment I encouraged (eg two current directors of large companies started with me as junior staff).'

'A high degree of autonomy. As a director once mentioned to me, his job was to often aim the rifle, my job was to be the bullet that was fired out and rapidly hit the target. He wouldn't or shouldn't have to make major alterations, rather through coaching, discussions and advice, slightly nudge the direction of the bullet (ie me). I see myself performing this type of role for people who report to me.'

'I don't mind being managed if my work stream and ownership of that work stream are clear. Managing others is key to testing and refining your own creative ideas and style, but I need adequate time to coach and manage others. I get frustrated just handing out orders. A creative person also requires quality alone time, not persistent team interaction.'

For many it was not something that they really wanted to do, either because they had no real interest in it, or as a number of respondents said, as they got older they wanted to do it less.

'I've done this and been good at it but I really like not doing so.'

'Have previously managed a small team of people. My personal difficulty comes with confrontation; I like to work with consensus as opposed to an "iron hand".'

'As much as it takes to get the job done – responsibility comes from what I do not from what I am granted or given.'

'After 25 years of doing it, I'd rather not be bothered any more! I like working with self-motivated self-starters who I can trust to get on with it.

I no longer have any patience for all the little mundane personnel hassles that are involved in organizations.'

'I only need to retain a very limited amount of control but I do want to be sure that everyone involved understands my vision. The end result might not be exactly what I had imagined but the input from others along the way should help to polish the core idea.'

As well as asking individuals about how they liked to manage there was also a question about what management style they would prefer and there was an unquestionably united response to this:

'Enabling and empowering. "Go do it and **** up if you need to" was one of the best pieces of advice I ever got.'

'Motivational – Herding – Charismatic – Exploratory – Time for Everyone – Confident Visionary.'

'Informal coaching and entrepreneurial.'

'Light touch. Am a self-starter.'

'A true coach... one who allows a round table and good feedback with support.'

'I really hate being managed so the best management style is one that agrees what's needed and then trusts me to deliver.'

'Trusting and hands-off, where talent is valued, with positive tolerance of diversity and ambiguity.'

Others emphasized the importance of a balanced approach, wanting some direction or guidance and then to be left alone but still to feel that their manager was interested and able to offer support if needed:

'Hands-off; available; support AND challenge (in that order).'

'Very clear objectives, balance risk and prudential judgement.'

'Agree a desired outcome, contract the terms and conditions and leave me to it, but stay interested.'

'Challenging, decisive, calculated risk-taker, team orientated, values input, not control orientated.'

'Definitely empowering, often criticized in the past for not being involved enough (not by my staff I hasten to add, but by those above me!). Trust that the people I have recruited can do the job and will call if they need me. Then I can be a coach or instructor depending on the needs of the individual.'

'Trusting, supportive and unobtrusive.'

Some also emphasized the importance of working in teams citing self-managed teams as a preference:

'Definitely team... I really believe in forming, norming, storming, performing and also like Belbin.'

'Unbureaucratic and non-hierarchical. Flexible teams are important.'

'Leaders that model the behaviour they expect from their teams – leaders that are committed to growing other people.'

One respondent said:

'Ask for forgiveness, not permission.'

CREATING A DEVELOPMENT PLAN FOR TALENTED INDIVIDUALS

One of the challenges can be creating appropriate learning for talented individuals. Increasingly, organizations are moving away from menu-driven training to more competence-based learning. In the model below, individual learners are encouraged to ask themselves questions, to reflect on their experiences as part of their learning. This self-assessment and reflective learning however does need support from either a line manager or coach.

What follows is a sample of a competence-based development plan about being enterprising.

Generates novel ideas, avoids early conclusions

▌ How regularly do I take time out to broaden my horizons?

▌ When was the last time that I was really creative? How many of my ideas did I put into practice? How effective is my idea generation process?

▌ How open is my mind? How often do I say 'Why don't we try this?' versus 'We've tried it before, it won't work'?

▌ How often do I spend too long thinking and not enough time actually doing?

▌ How can I formulate my ideas so that I can share them with others?

▌ Who do I know who thinks differently from me, what could I learn from them?

▌ How creative am I? Not everybody naturally comes up with novel ideas or original thought, but it is possible to improve your idea generation process. Be hungry for information, be curious. Take opportunities to be creative, write, draw, take up creative hobbies.

▌ Give your mind freedom to explore.

▌ Take the opportunity to brainstorm with others, allow your mind to explore the unexpected, take away some of the constraints on your creativity. Use creative techniques, like word association, mind-mapping®, using sticky notes, 'blue-sky' thinking to push the boundaries of your mind.

▌ Share ideas with others. Companies like Disney use a technique called 'displayed thinking' where ideas are incubated by a continuous process of brainstorming when the originators of the ideas allow others to add their input. Take advantage of global time zones to work virtually in teams through e-mails.

▌ Use idea generating techniques to ask yourself the following: What other uses could we have for this? What do our customers need that we don't currently give them? What do we have that works really well that could be adapted? What could we do quicker? More efficiently? Listen to others; don't close down too early. Even if a good idea is not used, capture it, as it may prove useful at a later time.

▌ Take time to identify what really inspires you. Where do you go to stimulate your creativity? How often do you take time out just to think, what opportunities do you take outside of work to see, or take part in creative activities? Visit art galleries, museums, theatre and concerts.

Identifies and explores wider, less obvious options in a situation

▌ Lateral thinkers generate ideas without judging their merits. They often challenge conventional ways of thinking. There are techniques that can help stimulate lateral thinking, eg Edward de Bono books/courses, Buzan's mind-mapping®. Lateral thinking will eventually lead to you reaching a conclusion, but not necessarily in a logical, step-by-step manner. It generates a wealth of ideas by pulling down barriers and encourages people to think around a problem.

▌ Practise lateral thinking; identify tools and techniques to help you think more creatively.

▌ Find out about your preferred learning style, recognize how you problem solve currently. Experiment with using different techniques to build your creativity.

▌ Identify others who have a different natural style perspective and try to understand the logic behind their thinking. Ask questions and ask them to share their thought processes.

▌ Build teams of people with different styles of thinking; take time to explore how you can work together and how the process would work. Recognize that some people demonstrate creativity in working within the structure of the organization, while others will want to work more with the idea generation process. Play to people's strengths.

Is intrigued by new concepts and leverages them to gain business advantage

▌ Successful entrepreneurs are always on the look out for new ideas and business concepts, and opportunities to create something new. They scan the marketplace looking for ideas that they can imitate or improve. Assess the marketplace: who are the originators? Who are the imitators? What are the advantages of being first to market? How could you apply what you find out within your organization?

▌ When faced with a problem within your group encourage the team to think creatively around the problem. Use creativity techniques like brainstorming and SWOT (strengths, weaknesses, opportunities and threats). Strengths and weaknesses usually apply to current and internal factors, opportunities and threats to future and external influences. Come up with new ways of handling traditional problems.

▌ Do not cling to the past, become an 'early adopter' of new ways of working, be prepared to experiment with ways of working differently.

▌ Spot new trends, be prepared to analyse their potential application on behalf of the team.

Develops further, implements and embeds new ideas, processes or products

I The incubation of genuinely new products or processes may not be easily achieved within the normal production schedules of a large organization. Explore creative ways of developing a test-bed environment. Consider alternative methods of simulating production.

I Share ideas with your colleagues and develop teams of entrepreneurial thinkers who can explore new innovation. Develop a template of screening questions, which will help present the innovation to the business: How does this fit with our overall business strategy? Is it consistent with our organization brand? What advantages will it bring for our customers? Why has it not been done before?

I Not all ideas need to be new, so do not 'reinvent the wheel'; take time to recognize what already works well and find ways of developing this further, or find new ways of using existing ideas within the business. Follow ideas through carefully to the implementation stage, taking note of the progress and issues at each stage. Once implemented, regularly monitor for success.

Takes calculated risks

I Examine your area of the business and develop scenarios for how it could develop over the next three years. Explore the best/worst/most likely outcomes. Ask a colleague to do the same and compare results.

I Develop your own and your team's acceptance and tolerance level for the unfamiliar and unexpected. Break the work routine. Try different approaches. Have the courage of your convictions to see things through. People who are courageous confront difficult situations rather than withdrawing to safe ground. They use their experience and judgement to manage risk appropriately. How courageous are you? Are you someone that can be relied upon in a crisis? How resilient are you?

I Take responsibility for systematically accounting for and promoting responsible risk-taking that is relevant and in context. Always think through the consequences of a 'Just do it' approach.

I Do not be afraid of taking decisions, but use clear and well-publicized criteria, be fair and consistent, be prepared to discuss the reasons for your decision.

Offers independent ideas. Challenges the status quo

I Use creative thinking to generate new ideas, execute a strategy for promoting and exploring the viability of these new ideas with others whose view you respect.

I Make sure that ideas are not prematurely shut down. When ideas do not work out as planned take the opportunity to review the reasons for the lack of success. Make a habit of asking, 'How would I do it differently next time?' Invite and listen to the ideas from new or younger employees, who may challenge the status quo.

I Do not always give up on an idea if it hasn't worked the first time: good ideas often fail to be adopted initially. With careful planning and analysis it is possible to re-present an idea more successfully on a second occasion.

I Be prepared to champion an idea that you passionately believe in. Work to maintain sponsorship throughout the lifecycle of the idea.

I Identify colleagues with a different viewpoint whose opinion you trust to review your idea and to give you critical feedback. Keep putting your ideas through rigorous testing.

Turns creative ideas into effective business solutions

I Don't just have a good idea; follow it through to a commercial solution that adds value to the business. Take time to work through the business implications. If you really believe that it is a viable business proposition, put together a business case.

I Some entrepreneurs have difficulty in translating their vision into a strategy for implementation; find others who are capable of supporting you to move your idea from dream into reality.

I Identify managers within the business who would be effective mentors or sponsors of your ideas. Regularly meet with them to update them on progress and to use them as a sounding board.

I Extend your network outside work; meet with other successful entrepreneurs, read case studies of people in a range of sectors who have achieved business success. See if you can identify common factors.

Other development questions

Ask yourself the following:

I How creative are you? What actions do you take to generate new ideas?

I How do you encourage others to accept what is new and different?

I Do you come up with unconventional solutions to ongoing problems?

I How easy is it for you to spot connections and linkages between apparently unrelated factors?

I How often do you discuss issues with colleagues outside of your function and ask for another viewpoint to help you find a solution?

I Do you allow yourself time to consider all the issues, explore all possibilities and consult with stakeholders when making key business decisions?

I How far do you look ahead when considering the possible impact of business decisions? What actions do you take to think laterally and strategically?

I How many contacts across the business do you have? How successful are you at maintaining those contacts?

I If you could implement one major new idea, what would it be?

You may want to discuss some of these questions with another team member, your manager, or someone outside work.

The above development plan indicates one way of encouraging individuals to take responsibility for their own learning. It could also form part of a blended learning solution. The case study below highlights how an organization can create an ethos to help talent thrive.

IN SUMMARY

I Talented people are often complex, and do not necessarily understand themselves what they want, as they are in a continual process of growth. As some of our earlier feedback has revealed, sometimes they drive and drive to get something, only to find when they finally get it they have lost interest in it.

I   How we learn is one of the most individual and personal activities that we ever undertake and yet most of us spend most of our learning lumped together in learning environments which give us very little opportunity for individual coaching and support. For creative and innovative people, whatever their age, this is even harder. They crave feedback, they need time to reflect, they want very specific coaching to help them develop what they know they need to know. Unlike many others they often have a purpose to their learning and they get incredibly frustrated with what they may perceive as trivia, or irrelevant information.

I   Learning that means something important, personal and special to the individual will have far more impact than a generic learning product.

I   One of the challenges can be creating appropriate learning for talented individuals; increasingly organizations are moving away from menu-driven training to more competence-based learning. This self-assessment and reflective learning however does need support from either a line manager or coach.

3 MONKEYS CASE STUDY

What does your organization do to create a culture and climate to encourage the learning potential of all employees?

Like all consultancies of every discipline, we depend for our livelihood and very existence upon the commitment, loyalty and enthusiasm of our staff. Without their wholehearted and energetic application of brainpower and creative talent, our business would wither on the vine, so our fabric and culture is built exclusively around our people.

How do you attract, engage and retain talented people?

Sensibly, our recruitment policy stems from our business plan. We identify a defined role for the incoming consultant and brief recruitment agencies thoroughly in our goals, mission, corporate culture or 'religion' and the specific job description.

On appointment, we give every joiner a copy of the 3 Monkeys Bible, which outlines how we do things, who does what and how they fit into our world.

We sit down with each joiner and consult them on how they believe they can best add value and agree a set of measurable objectives.

Who drives the process and which departments were involved?

We have a dedicated HR director who has developed a set of policies to cover best practice in recruitment, career guidance, mentoring and staff development.

How have you managed the ongoing expectations of talented people?

Because we believe that each newcomer adds appreciably to our pool of creativity, we have an informal chat with them every month about their progress and their concerns, and this is also a great opportunity to hear their ideas for how they can improve our business.

In this company, training and coaching never stop. We identify company-wide and individual specific training needs every three months. In some instances these needs are met using internal training programmes (for example copywriting skills, media awareness, etc). At other times, external training is arranged (for example in the use of specialist software and radio promotion).

Uniquely, we have also introduced a 'show and tell' programme where individuals give a presentation on what they're working on or, in the case of new recruits, what they did before they joined 3 Monkeys.

What are the biggest challenges in managing talent within your organization and how have these been overcome?

3MC has already achieved outstanding success as 'New Consultancy of the Year' in 2005 because it has attracted a number of hugely gifted individuals. The board recognizes only too well its challenge to motivate and inspire these people and their newer colleagues as the years speed by. Nothing, nothing at all, is considered more vital than responding to that challenge.

What measures or processes have you put in place to measure the effectiveness of your talent strategy?

Every six months we hold a formal review process with each of our staff. We invite feedback from everyone's peers in addition to their clients. We give the appraisees the opportunity to say how they feel they've performed and what their suggestions are for improving. They're also asked to share any perceived barriers to success. All are given specific guidance on what they need to do to be given greater responsibility.

In terms of reward, we recognize that different people respond to different types of reward. Unsurprisingly, we learned some years ago that money isn't everything, though it helps! The opportunity for job satisfaction, great comrades and stimulating working conditions rank very highly indeed in the needs of people in the PR world.

What have been the benefits?

As a small company we remain sufficiently flexible to accommodate most specific needs. This means, for example, we help one team member with travel to work costs, while another is set up to work from home when needed. We've consulted each of the 'Monkeys' and asked what extra rewards would make their lives even happier at 3 Monkeys. This covers everything from 'duvet days' where people are allowed an extra day off on their birthdays, to a fish tank in our office!

As well as the company's Chief Monkey, Angie Moxham, its hugely experienced and inspirational leader, we have a non-executive director, Laurence Rosen, who in the 1980s pioneered programmes that set high standards in Corporate Enrichment Culture, Staff Mentoring and Investing in People in his nationwide recruitment company Office Angels.

About 3 Monkeys

3 Monkeys is one of the fastest growing communications consultancies in the UK. Its experience spans corporate, consumer and b2b campaigns with some of the best-known brands in the world. A full service PR consultancy, it provides most services within the communications mix: strategic communications planning, media relations services, key influencer programmes, promotions and competitions, event management, online and viral PR, media training, newsletter, brochure and report production. It works for companies across the UK, Europe and internationally. Its work has won

accolades, but more importantly, it has enhanced its clients' business and reputation.

Contact details: angie@3-monkeys.co.uk

8

Creating a talent pool

TALENT AND EMPLOYABILITY

As our research has shown, employing talented people is not necessarily an easy task, and for the individual, traditional patterns of employment also present challenges. One of the most fundamental challenges can be the depth and breadth of interest. For many talented people, the ideal solution for them would be to be employed for their brain, their creativity, their thoughts and ideas. Some employers do embrace this, but for many they prefer a more traditional approach.

Phillip Brown and Anthony Hesketh outline many of the issues in *The Mismanagement of Talent* (2004).

> 'Little short of a cultural revolution is required in the way organizations utilize the talents and capability of graduates and to meet the expectations of the latter for interesting and meaningful work. But the way companies organize their human resources and especially their approach to graduate recruitment cannot be explained solely as a functional issue of making sure that there are people with the appropriate knowledge and skills to fulfil the strategic mission of the organization...'

Rather than re-imagine the social organization of work, talent has to be redefined. Whereas it relied on expert knowledge and claims to innate superiority to justify privileged positions and rewards, legitimacy now rests on leadership and 'performativity' measured in terms of market value. Knowledge is part of a broader consideration of personal performance, captured in the idea of charismatic rather than bureaucratic personality. It is based on charisma, energy and creativity alongside any consideration of knowledge and know-how.

GROWING TALENT

So who needs to be involved and when?

This very much depends on the business and its internal structure. As a first step it is really important to understand and think through the implications of embarking on a process of talent development before figuring out the who and when. What are the immediate needs? What are the 'must haves'? Who will benefit in the organization and how will the organization as a whole benefit?

The following represents some key steps in creating a talent development process:

1. Strategic level discussion paper
    Importantly, when reviewing your approach to talent development you need to examine what already exists. Take what works in your organization and build on it. Take the lid off your organization and look inside. What do you see? What would make you unique and different? How can you build loyalty? Do you know what talent already exists?

    One of the major considerations in creating a talent development process is the ability to enable different parts of the business to talk to each other. As part of the background research it is important to capture a broad spectrum of views from the CEO and the board, senior and line managers, the current cadre of people who are considered to be talented and members of the HR team. Sample questions could be as follows:

    – How is talent defined and identified in this organization, ie what do we mean by talent?
    – How effective is our recruitment process at identifying talent?

- What does our organization do to create a culture and climate to encourage the learning potential of all employees?
- What steps have we taken to create an environment where potential employees want to come and work for us?
- How should we attract, engage and retain talented people?
- How is high potential identified and sponsored? What do we do to actively champion talent?
- What do we do to actively encourage experimentation and allow failure in pursuit of a good idea, or new ways of operating?
- What steps have we taken to ensure that our management structure is developing new talent and creating a coaching and learning culture?
- Is our performance management system flexible enough to recognize individual potential and to reward unique behaviour? If yes, how is this achieved?
- Do we have a diverse and multi-talented workforce? How has this been achieved?
- How have we managed the expectations of talented people?
- What measures or processes have we put in place to measure the effectiveness of our talent strategy?
- What is our policy on redeployment; what do we do to encourage talented people to return to our organization?
- What is the biggest challenge in managing talent within our organization?

The above is only a sample of some of the questions that could be used in your background research.

Use all this data to create a proposal for your senior manager and hopefully for your executive board. It is important that any paper that is prepared follows the principles of any business proposal and clearly lays out the options, the business/individual benefits, the likely costs and the proposed timescales. There should also be an executive summary.

It may also be possible at this stage to gain outside support in the form of benchmarking best practice. Initial discussions with suppliers can also help in positioning the internal business benefits in the context of either your business sector or the wider global community. In any communication it is always important to be mindful of your audience, but in this context it is even more important to make sure that the language used is accessible, and not full of jargon.

It is also important that whoever presents the paper should be passionate and enthusiastic, but also knowledgeable about the content and able to make a persuasive business case. It is also important to look at the costing of the proposal within the context of the other business priorities; working with suppliers about the proposed phasing of the costs can also be helpful. One vital component that is often missing is the presentation of the ROI potential or cost savings within the business case.

2.   Sponsorship from directors and buy-in from the executive
As highlighted above, if the potential has been carefully outlined with all the business advantages, it will be easier for the executive to commit to the development of talent. The hope should also be that talent development is an issue close to the hearts and minds of the CEO and all the members of the board. It will be helpful if as part of your interview process you have identified directors from the business as well as HR who are supportive of the need to develop a process for talent development. Do not underestimate the need to build the case for the executive; if the process involves investment it will be competing with a number of business drivers.

3.   Internal champion/coordinator appointed
Assuming the organization decides to progress a process of talent development well as the higher-level support, it will need an internal champion or coordinator who will be responsible for the day to day management of the talent development process. This person, or team, needs to be not just familiar with talent. As highlighted in the questions above talent development is a far-reaching process, and involves a number of functions and both internal and external providers. (See also Chapter 3: Becoming an employer of choice.)

4.   Discussion paper formulated into an action plan with clear accountabilities
Like any learning development initiative it helps to be able to articulate the key stages and to outline them in an action plan and importantly to allocate key accountabilities. In this context it will range across a number of areas from external recruitment marketing to individual personal development. If this action plan is linked to the planned expenditure and the potential outcomes it will help even more in managing the planned expenditure. Again this action plan needs to link to the overall strategic plan. It needs to be written clearly highlighting the key points, any jargon needs to be clarified and it needs to be set in a business context.

Also include a timeline in the action plan; do not underestimate the time it takes to implement certain solutions.

5. Undertake an audit of the current talent development process provision, analyse who is doing what to whom and create an action plan.

In examining the overall process of growing leaders, managers and expert talent for the future, these may be some of the tasks. Identify the following:

- base line competency-based criteria for the role of a manager and ways of identifying and developing management talent;
- additional stretch goal criteria that distinguish talent;
- an accurate analysis of the talent that currently exists and the gap between where you are and where you would like to be;
- a development plan to increase the opportunities for talent to be grown;
- a review of the current learning and development opportunities offered to managers;
- the identification of other opportunities for talented individuals within the business;
- the creation of a method and template for succession planning across the business for expert and leadership roles;
- identifying the key roles that need succession plans;
- setting up a process for tracking talent and identifying successors/talented individuals for those roles.

MANAGING THE IMPLEMENTATION OF THE TALENT DEVELOPMENT PROCESS

The role of the line manager

Increasingly line managers are being encouraged to play a role in talent management. Developing the 'macro-enabling' skills of facilitation, coaching and giving feedback could provide line managers with a set of core skills that can be used in a variety of situations. If as part of this development they are also encouraged to practise questioning, listening and observing they will feel better equipped to identify the real development needs of their team. Finding the right solution could be a combination of using internal and external provision, online learning and their own coaching support as the learner puts this into practice. It also means that they can regularly set goals and discuss the progress of the individuals within the team. Working in collaboration with others towards achieving team goals can be a powerful motivator for talented individuals.

Developing a coaching environment

As we have highlighted earlier the corporate world is changing quite dramatically, businesses are facing challenges on an unprecedented scale and the retention of key employees is a major ongoing challenge. Employees equally are looking for organizations that value their contribution. One major way of helping all individuals fulfil their potential is to develop a coaching environment. This is not something that will be achieved overnight, but if you can engender a sense of sharing wisdom you are more likely to create a real sense of personal development. This is very different from the process of 'managing' and could play a major role in the successful implementation of a process of talent development. A coach guides rather than manages; throughout history there have been instances of guidance being given by 'elders'. What if instead of creating 'managers' we created guides? What if we gave respect to the wisdom of our experienced workers? The very best supervisors and managers are those who share their wisdom and give guidance to new employees. The very worst managers are those who play it by the rules with no flexibility or explanation.

Introducing a coaching environment may have a very far-reaching impact; individuals need to think about their very best learning experiences, to remember what inspired them, to think about how they can recreate special learning. Managers need to forget about being in control; instead they need to help their team members to explore by asking open questions and being provocative, and, although individuals should never be taken unsupported outside their comfort zone, they can be encouraged to push their boundaries beyond their normal learning experiences. Equally, members of the HR function could also perform the role of a coach and may need to recognize that in the future training may become much more focused on the individual, and as a result small discussion groups or one-to-one coaching may occur more frequently than classroom sessions.

Create an environment where people want to work

One of the recent trends in employee development is a recognition that retention of key employees is going to become increasingly important. With reduced resources available, everyone is going to be competing for the same people. Graduates have excellent networks. On leaving university they keep in touch with each other and compare the offerings from different organizations.

As highlighted below, employees expect more from an employer than just a pay cheque at the end of each month. To a certain extent the UK lags behind the US in the facilities it provides for its employees, and given the hours that most people work, more could be done to create environments where people want to work. Flexible working, job-sharing, being more accommodating to mothers returning to work, and recognizing the different lifestyle and work/life balance requirements of all employees are just some of the actions that employers can take to create a more employee-focused environment. As nations, we are becoming more aware of the impact of diet and exercise, incorporating some of this philosophy into the facilities that are offered to employees. Along with a cleaner more airy environment, this means that employees not only want to work for you, but it is healthier for them too.

Recognize the importance of employee engagement

In Chapter 3 we discussed the importance of developing an employer brand. As part of that process it is also important to recognize how to engage with a diverse group of employees. The profile of the workforce is changing and the expectations, wants and needs are different than they were even 10 years ago. Organizations are increasingly focusing on what they need to do differently to retain _all_ employees, not just the talented ones. The cost of recruitment can have a significant impact on the bottom line, but more importantly if an organization has a poor retention reputation it manifests itself in a variety of ways. For example, in some service sectors it is common for a number of companies to operate in a similar geographical area. Within this area, employees often 'job-hop', taking the experience gained in one organization to move on to another. It may be because the money offered may be slightly higher, it may be because they follow their friends, it may also be because one company gains a reputation for being a 'better' employer.

Identifying what makes a 'better' employer is one of the more critical actions an HR department can undertake. Do you know where your company sits in the local league of employers? How do your past employees describe your company when they are on induction courses with your competitors? Employee satisfaction surveys have a mixed response within HR departments and from employees themselves. Creating well-structured questions, with clear improvement actions taken as a result of yearly feedback, can provide a useful measure of the level of employee engagement.

Another issue is retaining the knowledge worker. In today's organizations when a relatively small number of people are developing specialist skills, if these people 'walk' there is a very high risk of part of the business going with them. As far ago as in 1996 Brook Manville and Nathaniel Foote, in a *Fast Company* article entitled 'Strategy as if knowledge mattered', were predicting the following: 'The essence of successful knowledge-based strategies is a company's capacity to raise the aspirations of each employee. These are the people whose contributions and ongoing development becomes the life-blood of performance gains.' Today's younger employees are much more mobile than previous generations. In some cases organizations are offering financial incentives for people to join them, such is the need to attract new talent.

There are some common sense ways of engaging employees, and some of these have been mentioned in earlier chapters, such as:

I Think very carefully about the messages that you are sending out to potential new employees through your recruitment advertising.

I Recognize the opportunities that exist to create a positive employer brand through all stages from the moment you send the acceptance letter to them joining the company.

I Some organizations use the term 'onboarding' to describe a process of support for the new employee, which starts at pre-employment, continues to induction and follows through to the first few months of employment. Following the onboarding period, supportive management and ongoing constructive feedback is provided to maintain the employee's loyalty.

I Provide real opportunities for progression, new responsibilities, new teams and cross-functional working.

I Give clear and visible leadership and show each and every employee that they are valued in the overall delivery to the customer.

I Allow for the right development, the right resources and the right support to enable each employee to perform effectively.

I Ensure communications are clear, using all forms of media, to make sure the employee really feels knowledgeable about company performance.

I Play an active role in the community, ensuring the company is recognized for its corporate and social responsibility.

▌ Work and play together, have fun, recognize achievements and celebrate personal, family and company success.

Put people development high on the corporate agenda

In recent times there was talk of breaking through the glass ceiling, but perhaps equally important is breaking down the mahogany door on the corporate boardroom and helping the occupants recognize the importance of being committed to people development. As Goleman, Semler, Bennis and Biedermann and the McKinsey Consultants have highlighted, commitment to people development needs to start at the top of an organization; it is not just an issue for HR and training and development functions. The leadership behaviours set the tone and expectations for employees. People are smart, talented people are even smarter: they will be not be taken in by lip service to values, they want to see an active demonstration in the day to day people management of the business.

Give clear guidance on expectations and goal setting

Some of the very real issues, particularly for talented people, is time wasting, bureaucracy and trivia. Giving clear guidance on expectations and agreeing the specific details on deliverables means that individuals can really focus on what they need to do. Meetings can be shorter, objectives can be set and work can be completed within a shorter timeframe.

Train and develop line managers in coaching

The more collaborative and forward-thinking organizations recognize that a motivated workforce does not need to be 'managed' in the traditional sense. What talented employees do need is guidance, coaching and the sharing of wisdom. This was one of the five imperatives suggested in _The War for Talent_. Developing these coaching skills takes time and needs to be demonstrated through models of best practice that are cascaded throughout the organization. The implication of all this for organizations and trainers is a fundamental shift from training to learning: there is a distinct difference in ownership, the individual needs to own and take responsibility for their own learning, and there is huge importance in helping individuals realize their potential.

Use technology and flexible working to underpin activities

Despite huge advances in technology, companies are still comparatively slow in maximizing the potential that technology affords them. Today's workforce is exploring different options and opportunities, people are taking time out to travel, and they look for more flexible working patterns.

One of the distinct advantages of technology is the ability to transmit messages rapidly around the world. Globally, technological advances mean that organizations rarely sleep, working virtually. While Europe is asleep some businesses use the Pacific Rim, paying less for services provided by workers who are inducted into the culture of the country they are representing. Virtual team working means that talent can be shared globally. Technology can support flexible working; people no longer need to be in an office. For many talented people, freedom to operate is important: their creativity is unlikely to be contained within office hours. Allowing them flexibility and freedom will ensure that you maximize their contribution. New legislation related to work/life balance will mean that organizations will have to adopt a more flexible approach.

Be open about measurement and success factors

One concern that talented people often have is how their contribution will be measured. Equally, measures are not always shared with individuals. The organization may be using one set of criteria, while an individual believes that he or she is being measured against another set. This stage is very much linked to the goal-setting stage. Unfortunately many organizations still have annual appraisal systems that are not linked to the day to day activities of an individual. It is important that clear objectives are set, which are regularly monitored, and that individuals receive feedback and also have the opportunity to discuss their own view of their progress. In a coaching environment this will happen more naturally.

Create a reward and recognition system that is not just financial

There is a natural link between this stage and the stage above. Individuals do appreciate recognition for their achievements, being thanked for a particular action. Being given extra responsibility, being made to feel part of something special, are all valued by an employee. Financial rewards are important, but other forms of recognition are also important.

Create customer expectations; build relationships with suppliers, stakeholders and the community

Brand loyalty is created in many ways, but essentially it is all based on the relationships that an organization builds with its partners. Corporate social responsibility is becoming increasingly important. Features like the _Sunday Times_ 'Best Companies to Work For', Investors in People, and National Training Awards all emphasize the importance of these relationships. As highlighted in Chapter 3 no business can afford to ignore its standing in the community or with its customers.

HOW WELL DO YOU MANAGE YOUR TALENT?

Rate your process for talent management, and contrast your approach to those applied within our case study examples:

1. Have we developed a definable organization brand?

2. Do we actively demonstrate our values and brand in the way that we conduct our business?

3. Does this equally apply in the way we handle our people?

4. Are we committed to identifying and recognizing talent at all levels in the organization?

5. Do we have an infrastructure that allows individuals freedom to innovate, generate ideas and receive feedback?

6. Are we sure that our management structure is developing new talent and creating a coaching and learning culture?

7. Have we created an environment that attracts potential employees to want to come and work for us?

8. Do we welcome previous employees back?

9. Do we recognize the need for some employees to go?

10. Do we give honest, open and supportive feedback on performance?

11. Have we created internal forums that allow for healthy debate and discussion?

12. Do we undertake effective benchmarking with other organizations?

13. Do we know our retention rates?

14. Do we conduct exit interviews with all employees?

15. Do we encourage all our employees at all levels to identify other potentially talented people to join our organization?

16. Do we actively share our experiences and demonstrate best practice to other organizations?

17. Do we have a diverse and multi-talented workforce?

18. Do we share our expectations of each other?

19. Do we actively champion talent?

20. Do we see talent management as one of the core pillars of our organization development?

IN SUMMARY

❙ It is really important to understand and think through the implications of embarking on a process of talent development before figuring out the who and when. What are the immediate needs? What are the 'must haves'? Who will benefit in the organization and how will the organization as a whole benefit?

❙ Importantly when reviewing your approach to talent development you need to examine what already exists. Take what works in your organization and build on it. Take the lid off your organization and look inside. What do you see? What would make you unique and different? How can you build loyalty? Do you know what talent already exists?

❙ Commitment to people development needs to start at the top of an organization; it is not just an issue for HR and training and development functions. The leadership behaviours set the tone and expectations for employees. People are smart, talented people are even smarter: they will be not be taken in by lip service to values, they want to see an active demonstration in the day to day people management of the business.

❙ The more collaborative and forward thinking organizations recognize that a motivated workforce does not need to be 'managed' in the traditional sense. What talented employees do need is guidance, coaching and the sharing of wisdom.

DEPARTMENT FOR TRANSPORT CASE STUDY

What does your organization do to create a culture and climate to encourage the learning potential of all employees?

The Department for Transport was created in June 2002 to focus on building a safe, reliable and sustainable transport system. David Rowlands, the Permanent Secretary, had a very clear picture of how he wanted the Department to develop:

> 'I want us to be an open, outward-looking organization, working well together and with our delivery partners; professional in all aspects of our business; clearly focused and understanding the contribution we need to make as individuals and teams. We aim to grow our own capability, making the most of the people who already work in the Department, and this needs a structured approach to developing talent, rather than simply leaving people to manage their own careers.'

The clear message from the top about the type of organization we want is supported by ensuring we have the right infrastructure (policies and procedures) to support managing talent and the learning and development process.

Processes

Individual development is an important part of the performance management process and the midyear review focuses on development. We are currently undertaking an IiP review to gain accreditation in our own right (the Department was previously accredited as part of DETR), to ensure that all divisions reflect best practice in developing staff.

The focus of our approach to development is ensuring development needs are identified and addressed at line manager level to ensure managers take direct responsibility for managing people and organizational capabilities.

There is not a 'one size fits all' approach as employees' needs and preferences for addressing them vary.

The focus next year will be to look at the new Professional Skills for Government agenda and assess how best we can support the acquisition and use of the new skill sets to support business delivery.

How do you attract, engage and retain talented people?

Attract

We have raised DfT's profile in Whitehall, through a variety of networks, including Whitehall Industry Group, Aurora Women's Network, various professional benchmarking groups and our own press office. We wish to attract a diverse workforce, so we have made all our external partners, especially head-hunters, aware of our commitment to diversity and we have revamped our recruitment strategy focusing on how we can give better information to candidates about what DfT does and the benefits of working for DfT.

We also make use of the Cabinet Office Graduate Fast Stream programme to ensure we attract young people into DfT. In 2005 we hosted an open day for the Cabinet Office for prospective Fast Streamers.

In addition, our policy is that all our interview selection panels are trained in competency-based non-discriminatory interviewing techniques. We are also using more assessment centres for key grades to ensure we are appointing on merit.

Talent pools

Twelve months ago we established talent pools, to ensure that the Department has a pipeline of future talent, as a large proportion of our senior team are approaching the current retirement age. We have established a series of talent pools at key career stages to fast track development of our more able staff. We have also established a development pool called Green Light for our black and minority ethnic staff, to ensure ethnic minority staff are not disadvantaged and have equal access to promotion and development opportunities. The pools do not guarantee promotion (we use assessment centres and interview boards for promotion), but provide staff with support to develop, access to stretching roles, and an appreciation of how the organization works via access to our top team.

Each talent pool has a senior sponsor for the pool, eg Director General or Permanent Secretary, who ensures that staff are meeting their individual development plans and support is given to staff who require a move to a different role to enable breadth of development.

Selection to each talent pool involves completing an application form outlining evidence against competing framework and stating how the organization and individual would benefit from their inclusion in the talent pool; this is followed by a selection interview and a development centre for those that successfully pass the interview stage. The purpose of the development centre is to fine tune development needs and enable group members to develop a support network.

Key stages in the talent pool process are: the introductory workshop, development centre, review meetings at 6- and 12-month intervals. Participants also have a number of coaching sessions. The individual, their line manager and coach initially sit down together and discuss the development needs and agree a development plan. They also have a review meeting at the end of the coaching sessions.

The Permanent Secretary and his Directors General champion the talent pool. David always kicks off the Green Light induction programme, which is aimed at identifying potential leaders by supporting the development of minority ethnic staff to enable them to meet their full potential. This programme has a slightly different programme of events but is also supported with coaching sessions.

Other champions have a variety of ways of engaging with their group: informal lunches, away-days, one-to-one meetings, attending review meetings. We are not prescriptive about how champions work with participants but allow them to work flexibly with the group to develop a way of working that is not contrived and is beneficial to all parties.

Engagement

In terms of engagement we use traditional staff surveys to see what people think about working for DfT. The 2005 survey was followed up with staff focus groups and we are now developing with staff action plans to address the issues identified. HR has not led this, responsibility for various themes has been given to DG to own and progress.

There are also open sessions at different locations, held by the Permanent Secretary and the top team a few times a year, to explain key messages to staff and give staff the opportunity to respond. This is backed up by weekly e-bulletins to keep staff informed of any changes. Staff have the opportunity to respond by e-mail to any weekly messages.

In addition, DGs/directors host informal open sessions to talk about key policy changes, so that staff understand what is happening in the department.

We also run events called Valuing Diversity promoting various religious and cultural festivals and educating staff on various aspects of diversity. We also will be running short lunchtime sessions inviting prominent leaders from the private and public sector to speak to our staff on leadership issues and their approach or other key management topics.

Staff are also encouraged to organize their own special interest groups and we have staff network groups for part-time workers, black and ethnic minority staff, the gay and lesbian group and disability group. Various groups are consulted on key issues affecting staff and given the opportunity to comment.

Who drives the process and which departments were involved?

HR drives and administers the process for talent pools but sift panels and selection panels involve directors and line managers; the selection process for the High Potential scheme (aimed at developing future directors and DGs) involves the Permanent Secretary and Director Generals. We also use an independent external assessor on all talent pool selection panels which helps us avoid the 'horns and halo' effect and ensures we assess on the base of evidence presented to us, not on pre-conceived ideas.

In addition, we use external suppliers to run the talent pool development centres and undertake coaching session. Line managers are, however, actively involved in the development process as they are supporting employees on a daily basis. All the managers who are involved in the talent pool process are properly briefed on their role and responsibilities and given the appropriate support and development to enable them to undertake their role.

Outside of the talent pool process, we also try to encourage managers to identify talent and develop staff through the normal management interaction with staff; some managers are better than others at achieving this.

How have you managed the ongoing expectations of talented people?

We encourage the line manager to take responsibility for talented people. They will have ongoing discussions with the individuals about their expectations, and if someone feels that they are not progressing as quickly as they hoped, their line manager will work with them to help them stay motivated. Additional support is available from the Learning and Development Team and the talent pool champions who are available for support and advice, and will resolve any blockages to development.

What are the biggest challenges in managing talent within your organization?

Those not in talent pools can feel that everything is being done for those in the talent pools. It is important to think about the rest of the employees and get managers to support the development of all employees.

How have these been overcome?

Our Learning and Development team make sure that staff and managers understand that development is for everyone and encourage all employees to take advantage of the development that is on offer. Better signposting of what's on offer and the link to our competency framework has made it easier for staff to decide what is appropriate for them.

We also make use of the Learning and Development coordinators who are located within each department and also notify staff of events such as the annual Learning and Development Open Forum where our external providers offer short taster sessions of courses and staff have the opportunity to see what is available and talk directly to providers. The forum is always opened by the Permanent Secretary, which demonstrates to staff the importance of development to the Department's ongoing success.

What have been the benefits of talent pools?

In the longer term we have a supply of people who are suitable for our succession plans and we have a coordinated programme of development. For individuals it improves their commitment and understanding of personal development and its importance to them and their teams. This is essential to change the culture of the Department. For the Department, we will get better candidates for promotion, who are 'job ready' and have more rounded people management abilities, and are able to get the best out of their staff by supporting continuous development.

This is the start of a journey; we will need to refresh our talent process continually to take into account business priorities and central government initiative. In terms of successes from our talent pools we have already had a few promotions and some staff are working on high profile projects for the Department, which would not necessarily have been considered for inclusion in the project team.

What measures or processes have been put in place to measure the effectiveness of talent strategy?

Our scheme has been running for almost 12 months so we are just approaching the evaluation stage. We are looking at a number of measures that are both quantitative and qualitative.

The quantitative KPIs include the numbers in each talent pool (actual against planned) and the cost of the development programmes (actual against projected).

The qualitative KPIs include the quality of various elements of the programme such as coaching (external) and support from the line, development centre, etc.

A mixture of questionnaires and interviews with participants, line managers and senior managers are used to collect information.

Ultimately we need to evaluate that the talent pool process does offer value for money and meets its objectives of providing DfT with skilled staff.

What advice would you offer?

Christine Bennett, Head of Talent Management and People Development, says:

> 'When I started to set up the process, I did my research, I spent time identifying what other models existed, and how companies in both the public and private sector were approaching talent management. I prepared a strategy paper for the board and a consultation paper for the managers once the board had agreed in principle to the scheme. I was able to use the consultation period to address the concerns of line managers early on and obtain buy-in. I wanted to create something that was fit for purpose and was acceptable to the organization. My advice to others would be, do your homework and be flexible in order to develop something that fits your organizational priorities and culture.'

About the Department for Transport

The Department for Transport's objective is to oversee the delivery of a reliable, safe and secure transport system that responds efficiently to the needs of individuals and business whilst safeguarding our environment.

The role of the Department for Transport is to determine overall transport strategy and to manage relationships with the agencies responsible for the delivery of that vision.

Contact details: Christine.Bennett@dft.gsi.gov.uk

9

Developing thought leadership

'I think, therefore I am.'

Descartes

'Human intelligence and intellectual resources are now any company's most valuable assets.' This is not a recent quote: Rich Karlguaard, editor of *Forbes ASAP* made the statement in 1993. Edvinsson and Malone make reference to this in *Intellectual Capital* (1997).

One of the fundamental shifts in employment patterns today is the growth of the 'knowledge worker'. This is a term used to describe individuals who contribute to the growth of the intellectual capacity of an organization. Knowledge workers create the innovations and strategies that keep organizations competitive.

In *Thinking for a Living: How to Get Better Performance and Results from Knowledge Workers* (2005), Davenport suggests that companies continue to manage this new breed of employee with techniques designed for the Industrial Age. As this critical sector of the workforce continues to increase in size and importance, he suggests that it is a mistake that could cost companies their future. He argues that knowledge workers are vastly different from other types of workers in their motivations, attitudes and need for autonomy. Although some descriptors of knowledge workers might imply these are all young people, it equally applies to older employees who on finding themselves with fewer financial commitments, decide that they want to fulfil some lifestyle ambitions, and consequently leave organizations taking with them a wealth of experience and expertise.

Talented and high-performing knowledge workers are even more significant in today's mobile economy; these individuals are enormously valuable to organizations. As Davenport suggests, and we have mentioned in earlier chapters, these individuals are more likely to make choices based on meeting very different criteria.

Although money is important, it will not be their prime motivator. Flexibility in working patterns will be a driver, as will recognition and intellectual challenge underlying, therefore in this chapter we explore some of the principles around thought leadership and how you can help to develop a 'thinking' organization.

KNOWLEDGE MANAGEMENT

'Information equals power' and in today's organizations when a relatively small number of people are developing specialist skills, if these people 'walk' there is a very high risk of part of the business going with them.

Today's younger employees are much more mobile than previous generations. In some cases organizations are offering financial incentives to join a company such is the need to attract new talent. Being enterprising is no longer a term just used for people who want to run their own businesses; people need to be enterprising within their own organizations.

Some of the definitions of knowledge management describe how to develop systems to manage knowledge, in the same way as you might want to keep track of intellectual capital, but the most important factors behind knowledge management is what people keep in their own head.

Increasingly people are recognizing the importance of IPR (intellectual property rights). In previous generations individuals who created new learning concepts were only too happy to just have their findings published; now those same findings could have a value attached to them.

In a *Fast Company* article by Brook Manville and Nathaniel Foote, 'Strategy as if knowledge mattered' (1996), they identify the following as key steps:

1. Knowledge-based strategies begin with strategy, not knowledge.

2. Knowledge-based strategies aren't strategies unless you can link them to traditional measures of performance.

3. Executing a knowledge-based strategy is not about managing knowledge; it's about nurturing people with knowledge.

4. Organizations leverage knowledge through networks of people who collaborate – not through networks of technology that interconnect.

5. People networks leverage knowledge through organizational 'pull' rather than centralized information 'push'.

They conclude by suggesting that:

> 'The essence of successful knowledge-based strategies is a company's capacity to raise the aspirations of each employee. These are the people whose contributions and ongoing development becomes the life-blood of performance gains.'

WHAT ARE THE IMPLICATIONS OF BEING A THOUGHT LEADER?

To be a thought leader you need to be expressing thinking that is original and different; it requires maturity, a confidence and a self-belief, which will establish your reputation as having something of value to say. In a knowledge-based economy, size is irrelevant: increasingly large organizations are learning from SMEs. A number of our case studies illustrate how entrepreneurial young people have taken an idea and built businesses that have allowed them to create very different working environments. More and more talented people are moving into freelance positions, where they can share their creativity with a number of organizations and in doing so, create their reputation.

Talented people are often curious and they want to push the boudaries of discovery. To be a thought leader you need to be excited and energized by leading the field. You do not necessarily have to have come up with the original thought, but you do need to be able to grasp an idea and run with it.

WHAT ABOUT ORIGINAL THOUGHT?

One of the really interesting areas is original thought, which is often very hard to achieve. One of the reasons for this is that we often do not create the right environment for originality, or quite believe that we are capable of original thought. Like our intuition, or 'gut' reaction, original thought can be perceived as being a bit 'scary'. We may find ourselves with what we believe is an original thought and then we may be anxious because we have limited experience of being original.

This is the basis of true innovation: that 'aha' moment when you are faced with an opportunity that may bring competitive advantage, an advance in medical treatment, or just provide you with the opportunity to do something completely different with your life. If you do believe that it is an original thought, or a development of an original thought, you need to read all round it, become absorbed in it and allow yourself the space to explore it fully. In today's world of global communications there are excellent opportunities for you to share your views, knowledge and expertise.

Again this is the point at which you need your support network: people you can really trust to share your idea. Above all have self-belief: being original is not easy and you need a level of resilience to keep going with an idea when others may not see its value.

When is it the right time to share thoughts with others?

Always be careful with your intellectual property; increasingly it has a value.

What is important is that you share the right thoughts at the right time, because if sometimes we share our half-formed thoughts too soon, other people can put a negative influence on us and dampen our enthusiasm. However, we often need a sounding board, someone that we can trust, to share our first embryonic ideas. As part of your support network, identify people who can give you balanced feedback, who will help you explore your hopes, dreams and aspirations.

If you take your thinking seriously, others will equally begin to develop respect for your knowledge.

In *Intellectual Property* (2001), a business guide produced by the CBI and KPMG, there is a useful article by Eastwood and Zair examining how companies can seek to be proactive about their IP assets. They suggest that there are a range of questions that CEOs should ask themselves.

One of the most critical is an analysis of what IP exists in the organization, where it is held and how it is protected. They suggest that very few organizations would be able to answer the question with any degree of certainty. The value of intellectual property is becoming increasingly important, and organizations are finally waking up to its importance.

SO HOW DO YOU DEVELOP THOUGHT LEADERSHIP?

In Chapters 6 and 7, we explored some of the underpinning principles of creative thinking. In the Being Enterprising development module at the end of Chapter 7 we suggested some key actions in idea generation, eg:

▌ Taking time out to broaden your horizons.

▌ Be hungry for information, be curious.

▌ Give your mind freedom to explore.

▌ Take the opportunity to brainstorm with others.

▌ Use creative techniques, mind-mapping®, use blue-sky thinking to push the boundaries of your mind.

▌ Sharing ideas with others: use 'displayed thinking' to incubate ideas.

▌ Use idea generating techniques.

▌ Practise lateral thinking.

▌ Build teams of people with different styles of thinking.

▌ Assess the marketplace, look for the originators. What do they do differently from your organization?

▌ Do not cling to the past: spot new trends, become an 'early adopter' of new ways of working.

▌ Recognize that not all ideas need to be new, do not 'reinvent the wheel', take time to recognize what works well, be prepared to build on the ideas of others to create new.

▌ Make sure that ideas are not prematurely shut down; make a habit of asking 'How could we do it differently'? Invite and listen to the ideas of younger employees who may challenge the status quo.

▌ Be prepared to champion an idea that you passionately believe in.

▌ Don't just have a good idea, follow it through to a commercial solution.

Creative people enjoy thinking. Often used to spending time on their own, they can be more introverted than others, and sometimes drift off into their thoughts for long periods of time. However, others find that they have less and less time for thinking. When did you last indulge in some thinking time? We don't mean the anxious 'trying to remember lists of information' type of thinking, but real quality reflective thoughtful time, when you immersed yourself in thought so deeply that you had to almost physically drag yourself back to the present.

Following a sequence, exploring options, allowing incubation time are important parts of the creative process. Creative thinking time is a very precious commodity; allowing yourself time each day to explore ideas and new projects is critical to organizational and personal growth. Taking time out to think, to coordinate ideas and chains of thought, and re-order into coherent actions is something that many of us rarely find time to do.

> 'Less than 15 per cent of the people do any original thinking on any subject.... the greatest torture in the world for most people is to think.'
> Luther Burbank in *Great Quotations*, George Seldes

In order to take thinking seriously we need to prepare and to create thinking time. It is also important to try to clear some of the unwanted debris that is cluttering up our minds. One important fact is how much oxygen our brain needs to operate effectively; our brains amount to 2 per cent of our body's weight but consume 25 per cent of the body's oxygen intake, which is a very sobering thought when we consider the working environment for much of the world's workforce. How often in a working day do you go outside and find fresh air?

Many innovative and creative people started by playing a hunch, trusting their intuition and not being afraid to be first with an idea. Often they are then challenged by those around them to find proof that others think the same, rather than recognizing and acknowledging that perhaps it is an original idea. In all our research with talented people one of their biggest frustrations is the number of times they come up with original ideas and their partners or their organizations refuse to accept the validity of the idea and then when much later someone else develops it, it seems to be somehow more acceptable.

As individuals we all have the right to develop our own personal learning agenda. However much of a corporate person you are, your mind is actually your own. Developing your intellectual capability is the right of every individual and from a personal health point of view it is well recognized the more active you keep your brain the better it functions into old age, and there is some evidence that it can help to protect you against developing Alzheimer's Disease. It is, however, all too easy to neglect this aspect of your development. If your normal working day is full of responding to the demands of others it is very unlikely that you will feel that you are able to take time out to develop thought leadership, in fact achieving thought followship may be challenging.

If you want to develop thought leadership, it is important to learn to value your own contribution and to have the courage of your convictions. Equally, you need to find time to devote to research, or even just to create thinking time.

Marcus Buckingham in *The One Thing You Need to Know* (2005) makes a similar point:

> 'The best leaders I've studied all discipline themselves to take time out of their working lives to think. They all muse, they all reflect. They all seem to realize that this thinking time is incredibly valuable time for it forces them to process all that has happened, to sift through the clutter, to run ideas up the proverbial flagpole and then yank them down again, and in the end to conclude. It is this ability to draw conclusions that allows them to project such clarity.'

He gives the example of Sir Terry Leahy, Chief Executive of Tesco Plc, who refuses to carry a cell phone. 'He has identified his time in cars, trains and planes as his most productive time and he guards it jealously. Besides, he says "people know where I am going. They can reach me when I get there." '

This is endorsed by our research. In Chapter 4, when asked 'If you could change one aspect of organizations that would encourage the nurturing of talent, what would you recommend?', one of our respondents said 'For leaders to think.'

It is just as important to recognize that many of the greatest ideas emerge through an iterative process. Thomas Edison is quoted as saying, 'I haven't failed, I have found 10,000 ways that don't work.' Albert Einstein is attributed with stating 'I think and think for months and years. Ninety nine times the conclusion is false. The hundredth time I am right.' They are not alone: James Dyson, a modern day inventor, describes in his autobiography *Against the Odds* (1998) how he made hundreds and thousands of cyclones in the early days of inventing his vacuum cleaner.

HOW TO GENERATE IDEAS

In Chapter 6 and 7 we discuss some of the underpinning principles of creative thinking and idea generation. However, in the context of thought leadership, if you ever have been excited by a thought you will probably have discovered the process called 'flow' by Csikszentmihalyi (1990), a University of Chicago psychologist. He described this as the feeling when your mind develops a speed and pace of its own when you ignore meals or calls of others because you are so absorbed in the creative process. Writers, artists, musicians often experience this but it can happen to anyone in any sphere, if they learn to tune into their creativity.

The importance of flow is that the stream of ideas captured during this process is usually at a high level and deserves attention. By tuning into your flow of ideas, often in a short space of time you can create something which is of much more value than unproductive time spent staring at a computer screen or a blank piece of paper. Unfortunately, the feeling of flow can be elusive. With experience you can develop ways of stimulating flow, but for others it can be a frustrating process.

Earlier we referred to Gelb's book, *How to Think Like Leonardo da Vinci* (1998), which presented a host of ways of stimulating an individual's creativity. We mentioned one of his principles, *curiosita*, and how Leonardo da Vinci carried a notebook with him at all times, and that as a child, Leonardo possessed intense curiosity about the world around him.

> 'Great minds go on asking confounding questions with the same intensity throughout their ideas. Leonardo's childlike sense of wonder and insatiable curiosity, his breadth and depth of interest, and his willingness to question accepted knowledge never abated. *Curiosita* fuelled the wellspring of his genius throughout his adult life.'

Thought leadership is very much generated through curiosity, asking questions, exploring options, following trains of thought.

KEY ACTIONS TO STIMULATE THOUGHT LEADERSHIP

As part of a piece of research for an earlier book, *Managing the Mavericks*, we asked people for their sources of inspiration. The respondents in the survey had a whole range of sources of inspiration, often focusing on the senses. Creativity is rarely something that encourages you to stand on the sidelines; people who are interested in discovering their creativity usually jump in with both feet, as these extracts illustrate. Here is a sample of their responses:

'Books, history, media, individuals who demonstrate abilities and the results I aspire to. I also believe I have inner sources of inspiration, call it willpower, intuition, or spirit.'

'Time – Myself – Others – Inspirational People – Motivators – Those that live according to their own espoused values – Those that be rather than do.'

'Music, clean architecture and environment, books, movies, travel.'

'People – challengers and those not happy to accept the status quo. Bright sunny days and views of water!'

'For business creativity we use a lot of excursions, both linear and lateral, to stimulate ideas. At home inspiration comes from being in nature, meditating, doing yoga and reading.'

'Film, internet, philosophy and young people.'

'Absolutely everything on the planet could be a source of inspiration *or* a distraction.'

'Everything I've read, everyone I've met, everywhere I've been...some more than others, of course.'

'Inspirational moments in life. This may either be something in nature, music, something I've read, an actual event. I think this mainly relates to situations in which I see the hidden strength, the focus of conviction, beating the odds, excelling all these types of things.'

'Anything new, a place I haven't seen before, a picture on a card/postcard, a quote I haven't heard before, lyrics in songs, videos, stories in books/magazine articles, driving with nothing on my mind and suddenly a thought comes in that is somehow everything I have been waiting for but didn't know it.'

'Events, other people, but mostly "voices" in my head!'

'Books, pictures, images, songs, landscapes, memories, connections, others.'

'Thinking time and believing anything is possible.'

'Me, intuition and insight. About five people with whom I share ideas regularly and several people who've just surprised me! One of my staff out of a team of five. Reading, but less so as I get older.'

'Writing, reading, serendipity.'

'I am stimulated by anything visual and other creative people.'

WHAT ARE THE IMPLICATIONS OF THOUGHT LEADERSHIP FOR HR?

Developing thought leadership is not only important for the business, it is important for the HR function. In Chapter 2 we discussed the role of HR and described some of the issues for the HR function in today's changing organizations. One way that HR can work more effectively, not just in the role of business partner, but also in any relationship with its customers, is by focusing on developing its skills in thought leadership. It is a very valid role for HR, not just in carrying out risk assessment in areas of compliance but also in identifying leading edge research in people development. Every year in most countries there is the opportunity to enter your organization for an ever-increasing number of business awards. An important part of the judging criteria is often innovation. Identifying innovative ways of developing people, trying to do things differently is an important role for HR.

However, there is another reason for exploring thought leadership, which is for your own curiosity, personal development and growth in personal expertise. In Chapter 2 we highlighted the roles for HR as suggested by Ulrich and Brockbank and one of these roles was 'functional expert'. Here is a great opportunity to demonstrate thought leadership at least within your own organization, even if it is not on a broader national or international stage. If you are ambitious, however, starting with your own area of specialism, researching it and developing new theories is a significant step towards developing thought leadership on a larger scale. Equally, supporting the creative and innovative people within your organization is another important role.

One of the very real challenges for HR and L&D professionals is how to devote time to thought leadership. Operationally within the function the roles tend to be reactive, rather than proactive. Individuals find themselves in a situation where they are responding to the demands of the business rather than setting their own agenda. This is important too, because if you detach yourself too much from the business it is very easy to find yourself in a position where the business feels that you are not responding to their needs. Importantly, thought leadership needs to be balanced against pragmatic deliverables. In many beleaguered HR functions thought leadership couldn't be further from the way they respond to the day to day requirements of the business.

However, there will be times and opportunities when you can offer solutions to the business that can be interesting, leading edge and different. Achieving this often requires preparation and building a power base of recognition.

> 'I said to myself, I have things in my head that are not like what any-one has taught me, shapes and ideas so near to me – so natural to my way of being and thinking, that it hasn't occurred to me to put them down. I decided to start anew, to strip away what I had been taught.'
>
> Georgia O'Keefe

IN SUMMARY

▌ 'Information equals power' and in today's organizations when a relatively small number of people are developing specialist skills, if these people 'walk' there is a very high risk of part of the business going with them.

▌ To be a thought leader you need to be expressing thinking that is original and different. It requires maturity, a confidence and a self-belief, which will establish your reputation as having something of value to say.

▌ Today's younger employees are much more mobile than previous generations. In some cases organizations are offering financial incentives to join a company such is the need to attract new talent. Being enterprising is no longer a term just used for people who want to run their own businesses; people need to be enterprising within their own organizations.

▌ Talented people are often curious and they want to push the boudaries of discovery. To be a thought leader you need to be excited and energized by leading the field. You do not necessarily have to have come up with the original thought, but you do need to be able to grasp an idea and run with it.

▌ One of talented people's biggest frustrations is the number of times they come up with original ideas, and their partners or their organizations refuse to accept the validity of the idea and then when much later someone else develops it, it seems to be somehow more acceptable.

▌ Importantly, thought leadership needs to be balanced against pragmatic deliverables. In many beleagured HR functions thought leadership couldn't be further from the way they respond to the day to day requirements of the business. However, there will be times and opportunities when you can offer solutions to the business that can be interesting, leading edge and different.

Chapter 11 provides illustrations of people sharing their thoughts about talent.

10

The future for talent development

In Chapter 2 we raised the challenges faced by HR in becoming an effective business partner. We would like to end with a great example of one HR professional who has not only been recognized for his HR expertise, but also for his business contribution. Rusty Rueff was, until November 2005, senior vice president of HR at Electronic Arts, the world's largest interactive entertainment software company with revenues of over US $3 billion. In addition to overseeing global human resources and talent management at EA, Rueff was responsible for corporate services and facilities, corporate communications, and government affairs, but above all he had gained the elusive seat for HR at the strategic table.

In a 2001 *Fast Company* article by Anna Muoio, Rueff was interviewed about his approach to talent. He said:

> 'Creative talent is the scarcest resource on the planet. The primary limiting factor on our business is having enough creative leaders on our team. The challenge then becomes how to come into contact with the best of the best and how to establish relationships with them. If we can do that, then somewhere down the road – I might not know exactly when or where – they will work with us. If you build and nurture those relationships, you just know that it's going to happen.'

He believed that the real power is in high touch:

> 'In today's marketplace, people don't want to be treated like a commodity. They want to know that someone cares about their dreams.'

As well as his success with volume recruiting, elsewhere in the article it talks about him establishing global networks to identify talented people and how EA created a 'Top 40' list – a hit list of the most talented people throughout the world who, EA hoped, would one day work with the company.

The interview was carried out in 2001, and in November 2005 as confirmation of his talent as a business partner, Rusty Rueff joined SNOCAP as chief executive officer.

An extract from the press release was as follows:

> 'SNOCAP, the first end-to-end provider of digital licensing and copyright management services for the digital music marketplace, today announced its appointment of Rusty Rueff to the position of chief executive officer.
>
> 'As CEO, Rusty will continue to lead us on the path to achieving our company vision,' said Shawn Fanning, SNOCAP's Founder. 'Rusty's track record speaks for itself; not only has he demonstrated leadership by directing companies through significant growth but he has the desire, passion, and commitment that is a 'must' for SNOCAP.'

Rueff is an inspiring example to anyone who questions HR's capability to adapt to a business environment. His career wasn't particularly meteoric: he started his working life as a disc jockey, but unhappy with the transient nature of broadcasting he returned to university to study for a counselling degree. He is a great example of what you can achieve with passion and commitment.

WHAT WILL BE THE FUTURE TRENDS IN TALENT DEVELOPMENT?

The need to identify and develop talent is not going to disappear.

One of the interesting facts about today's working environment is that patterns of employment will never be the same again. Futurists in the US are researching how not just organizations, but also cities need to change to attract talented people to come and work in their environment. Individuals have a greater need for freedom and flexibility and a desire to create different patterns of working.

New patterns of working

In the UK, new directives such as DTI requirements about flexible working, the global emphasis on work/life balance and the need to address stress in the workplace, together with the growth of portfolio careers mean that organizations need to adapt to more flexible ways of working. The need to create flexibility in systems and ways of working that bring high rewards for high results may mean that people may spend less time in the office, but are far more productive.

Young people are more confident, more entrepreneurial; the more compliant generation of workers are retiring. There are fewer people in the workforce, who therefore have to be more effective and multi-talented. There are some common themes running through our case studies and our talent management survey and indeed in our findings from our other research. There were similar themes raised in *The War for Talent* (Michaels, Handfield-Jones and Axelrod, 2001)

These include:

I organizations taking ownership of their employer brand, staying close to the recruitment process in the search for talent;

I sending the right messages through words and deeds to encourage a diverse workforce to want to join your organization;

I ensuring that HR makes a full and positive contribution in the boardroom;

I better identification and retention of good talent;

I high-quality coaching by people with the ability and talent to coach;

I more self-management and mobility of talent in and between organizations and sectors;

I portfolio approach to managing careers;

I the need to develop flexibility in systems and ways of working, creating high rewards for high results, which may mean that people in fact spend far fewer hours in the office but are far more productive;

I staying connected with talented people, even after they leave, growing your network;

I empowering individuals to feel in charge of their own destiny;

I encouraging the release of energy and enthusiasm, saying 'we can' rather than 'we can't';

▌ making a positive contribution in the community;

▌ being open and committed to sharing best practice.

Here is a summary of the advice given from our case study examples:

▌ 'Anyone who is an internal working in learning and development is probably dealing with many of the same issues. My advice is to network like crazy with other colleagues in the business... blow down walls, initiate sharing best practices – inevitably it grows the talent pool for everyone.'

▌ 'Developing emotionally intelligent leadership, capable of sponsoring the potential leaders of tomorrow, will not happen overnight, but by building a team of senior managers who are capable of leading by example, inspiring and developing talent and who are able to give intelligent people permission and freedom to excel, will be a great start to the future development of leadership and talent.'

▌ 'There is a lot of talk about the need for empirical data but we believe that organizations should start when intuitively it feels right rather than hold back and wait for demonstrable business results.'

▌ 'Don't over-hype the organization or try to impose a corporate brand onto individuals by aggressively marketing a process of employer branding. We employ brilliant people so we nurture a culture which allows us to deliver on our values whilst still respecting their individuality. The focus should be on what we can do for them as much as what employees can do for us. Then we have a fighting chance of delivering to our brand promise.'

▌ 'Stay as close to talent as you possibly can. We keep a close connection with all our talented people; they receive coaching and mentoring from senior members of the business. Another important factor is that HR is closely connected with the business and people expect us to be involved in key business decisions.'

▌ 'Make sure you have commitment from the top – you need solid sponsorship to be maintained (especially when budgets are being reviewed and challenges unfold as you roll a programme out into the business). Make sure you have the right managers in people development roles – and measure their performance in that role. Aim, as we do, for the creation of an environment based on inclusive relationships that celebrate all successes – your own and others. To do this we have to promote a clear view of our market and our sharp understanding of what our clients feel and what drives them – these elements determine their needs and how to fulfill them. And we do not hoard this knowledge – it is not for a select few.'

▌ 'Grow talent, naturally and organically. From the very beginning one of our key strategies has been "Happy People" and this applies in all aspects of our business from employees to customers to anyone who comes in contact with their company. The three founder members enjoyed spending time with each other and they wanted to create an environment where everyone would enjoy coming to work. Yet behind this apparent informality there were also some very sound principles of people development. We encourage everyone to become an ambassador for the company; when they socialize with their friends they often share their enthusiasm about the company, and others have joined as a result of hearing about the style and culture of the company.'

▌ 'In terms of reward, we recognize that different people respond to different types of reward. Unsurprisingly, we learnt that money isn't everything, though it helps. Opportunity for job satisfaction, great comrades and stimulating working conditions rank very highly indeed in the needs of people.'

▌ 'When I started to set up the process, I did my research, I spent time identifying what other models existed, how companies in both the public and private sector were approaching talent management. I prepared a strategy paper for the board and a consultation paper for the managers once the board had agreed in principle to the scheme. I was able to use the consultation period to address the concerns of line managers early on and obtain buy-in. I wanted to create something that was fit for purpose and was acceptable to the organization. My advice to others would be, do your homework and be flexible in order to develop something that fits your organizational priorities and culture.'

As we are writing the final chapter of this book the world is commemorating the contribution of a highly talented musician John Lennon 25 years after his death. If there is one word that is associated with Lennon it is 'Imagine'. We would like to conclude with some thoughts about the future:

Imagine

When your employees...

Take responsibility for their own development. When they recognize the unique set of talents that they have developed and have the confidence to manage their own careers.

Are curious and develop the courage and wisdom to push against the corporate boundaries to make a difference within their organization, and in the wider community.

Become more self-aware and believe in themselves, when they eliminate negative self-talk. When they are able to generate optimism, take ownership of their development. When they respect the knowledge of others, are curious and want to share their own learning.

Are able to look to the future, to chart a journey and to keep on going towards their goals and take the opportunity to undertake their own development at a time, place and pace to suit them.

Are prepared to appreciate and value the contribution of others. When they recognize that if we give, we are more likely to receive. When they are able to develop empathy and commitment, and through developing a clearer understanding of their individual strengths and areas of development they can help their managers to support them.

When line managers...

Help people to use their imagination to dream and see alternative ways of doing things, of being innovative and creative, not being afraid to be first.

Develop a different set of core skills and emotional intelligence in order to identify, recruit and retain talent and to give honest, open and supportive feedback on performance.

Take responsibility for developing new talent, take time to coach and develop individuals on a one-to-one basis and select targeted, focused learning for their team members.

Use technology and other systems to undertake tasks that would otherwise be undertaken by individuals. Where trivial duties and non-essentials are stripped out of day to day activities.

Help people to want to help others help themselves, not being afraid to show they care. Are prepared to make a real contribution to their community.

A time when your organization is ready to...

Clearly define your employer brand and to recognize that talent management will be one of the core pillars of your organizational development.

Demonstrate your values and brand by creating a dynamic partnership between your employees and the organization, where individual skills and behaviours are aligned to corporate goals and objectives, and employees are supported as they work towards achieving their own goals, hopes and aspirations.

Create an environment that attracts potential employees to want to come and work for you, which also encourages and develops diversity within your workforce.

Be committed to and respect all your human capital. To also encourage flexible and imaginative patterns of employment. Where there are internal forums that allow for healthy debate and discussion. When individuals have freedom to innovate, generate ideas and receive feedback.

Ensure that your management structure is developing new talent and creating a coaching and learning culture. When it is committed to identifying and recognizing talent at all levels in your organization. When it is encouraging all employees to be committed to developing your talent pool. When it keeps track of talented employees who apply and may not be suited for the current role, when it encourages talented people who leave to return, if appropriate, at a later date.

Recognize how your corporate and social responsibility can enhance your employer brand and your links with the local community. Make an ongoing commitment to your community in deeds as well as donations.

When you are...

Inspired, excited, stimulated and motivated about not just the learning opportunities that you will create for others, but also the learning that you will undertake for yourself.

Able to network on a virtual and global basis, linking internationally with other forward-looking learning and development professionals.

Able to create your own best practice environment where you can build your own case studies based on the successes that you have achieved and the lessons you have learnt.

Able to make a difference and be part of a world class learning revolution that will change the way that talent is developed forever.

Imagine the future being now... it can be, if you and your organization have the commitment and drive to make it happen.

So how could you make a difference?

The reason why we wrote this book and why we believe that everyone so willingly took the time to complete the questionnaires and to take part in the case studies is that we care, not just mildly, but passionately, about people, the environment that they work and learn in and the right of every individual to fulfil their potential.

What puzzles us is why talent development is not higher on the corporate agenda and why some of the most blindingly simple strategies aren't in place to achieve this. Every comment made, every question asked is within the remit and power of most CEOs, executive boards and organization leaders. Most suggestions are linked to attitude and behaviour so the cost implications to the bottom line are negligible, but in terms of human capital the reward would be high.

We are not alone in our passion; some of the world's greatest companies have already demonstrated that focusing on developing the talent of all employees brings business success. Many of the writers already mentioned in this book have made similar impassioned pleas, but nothing will change until enough individuals with power and persuasion decide to really make a difference.

We live in uncertain times, we all have choices, leaders can choose whether they are really committed to leading, inspiring and caring about their people. Organizations can choose to come alive, recognize the real needs of their employees and set them free to contribute to the lifeblood of the organization. Individually we choose whether to share what we know, to help to energize others, whether to give, or to take.

The future for talent development has to be linked to creating a time and a place where every individual can give of their best. Within this environment it is also vital to recognize that certain individuals have the creativity and imagination to generate ideas and possibilities, which could create a world that is better for everyone. We owe it to them and ourselves to create a future that builds a diverse workforce, inspires everyone to make best use of their talent and sets organizations free from their bureaucratic shackles. Just imagine what a difference that would make.

All that remains is for us once again to thank everyone who contributed so willingly and so wisely to this book. Thank you for taking the time to read it. We hope you have found it interesting; whatever role you have in life, you have it within your power to help, assist, coach, lead, motivate, develop, or enthuse someone else.

'The people who achieve something truly unprecedented have more than enormous talent and intelligence. They have original minds. They see things differently. They want to do the next thing, not the last one...'

Bennis and Biederman, *Organizing Genius: The Secrets of Creative Collaboration (1997)*

We wish you every success in your journey of discovery. If you would like to contact us, we can be contacted on the following:

kaye@theinspirationnetwork.co.uk
andy@emergentedge.com

11

Talent – a personal view

TALENT – A PERSONAL VIEW: PETER HONEY

Peter Honey is a psychologist, author and management consultant.

1. **What is your opinion of how organizations in general treat talented people?**
   Not well enough. Organizations have a knack of suppressing the talents they need.

2. **How do you spot talent in a new group of employees?**
   By letting them 'go for it' and grow by learning from their mistakes.

3. **How did your schooling/initial approach to work impact on your talent?**
   Badly – it was as though there was a conspiracy to keep me in my place!

4. **What is the biggest challenge for talented people working in HR?**
   To escape from HR!

5. **Have you ever felt 'talent capped' in an organization? If so, what did you do about it?**

Yes, as I have already said, I certainly felt capped. My answer was to become a freelance as soon as possible and take control of my own destiny.

6. **What are the significant actions that organizations can take to nurture talent?**

To let go, to trust people to find a way and, above all, actively to support and encourage.

7. **How would you describe a talented person? Can you list some of the qualities, behaviours, competencies and the X factors that make a talented person different?**

Hmm... I think I'll cheat and attach a short article I wrote called 'What is talent?'

Extract below from 'What is Talent?' by Dr Peter Honey (October 2004) reproduced with permission from *The Training Journal*.

'The next day, when I met up again with my battered dictionary, I looked up the word we had banded around so glibly. Talent: innate mental or artistic aptitude (as opposed to acquired ability) less than genius. Now, as a behaviourist, I'm uncomfortable with anything that is described as innate. I much prefer things to be a) the product of learning and b) observable (like dear old behaviour!). So, I tried another dictionary hoping that it would drop the notion of talents being innate. Talent: natural ability to do something well. There it is again, "natural". I can feel the wretched nature–nurture controversy rearing its head yet again. Next I reach for *Roget's Thesaurus,* always illuminating, to find talent associated with words like intelligence, wisdom, gumption, capacity, brilliance and genius.

Next (I know, I know, it should have been first!) to Google to do an advanced search on talent. Up came an array of extraordinary websites. I find a list of talents covering aura reading, healing, water divining and aligning the matrix. I find a site urging people to use their gifts and talents to "enrich your life and the lives of others". It lists some talents that "people often have and don't even recognize as a gift or talent". Examples are: making others laugh or smile, creating something from nothing, making people and things beautiful, comforting others, inspiring and motivating others. I go on to read all about "dependable strengths" and the work of the late Dr Bernard Haldane, the originator of career counselling, who devoted his life to "challenging people to find out what they do well and how they can use their talents to serve the betterment of society". Now, totally hooked, I press on to find structured exercises designed to help people identify hidden talents.

Wow! Asking for a definition of talent is the equivalent of opening a can of worms. And to think that when I started, I was convinced that talents were skills by another name. But, the consensus of opinion suggests that a critical difference is that skills are *acquired* abilities whereas talents are *natural* abilities. But talents, I comfort myself, just like skills, still need to be identified, encouraged, nourished and developed. And despite all the evidence to the contrary, I still believe that a so-called "natural" talent only predisposes people to do something well and that, left to its own devices, starved of the opportunity to flourish, it could lie dormant and fail to materialize.

My search on the web inevitably turned up some quotes. How about this one? "I have no special talents. I am only passionately curious." Albert Einstein. Ah, but being passionately curious is probably a talent.'

8. **What advice would you give talented people who feel that they have lost their way?**
    Not to give up or become dispirited.

9. **Could you describe a perfect scenario when you really felt in tune with your talent, or in your ideal world how would you make best use of your talent?**
    Yes, when writing with the words flowing apparently effortlessly and, somehow, saying what I want them to say.

10. **Anything else you feel is important about talent?**
    Even though talents are apparently innate (see article) they still have to be developed before they can flourish and become recognizable as talents.

Contact details: www.peterhoney.com

TALENT – A PERSONAL VIEW: CAITLIN HAMMOND

Caitlin Hammond is a senior learning and development manager.

1. **What is your opinion of how organizations in general treat talented people?**
    It is difficult to generalize as it is still early days with structured talent management and many organizations are still trying to understand its true meaning and best application. I believe in the UK many organizations still tend to look at the technical attributes of talent rather than take a more holistic view of the individual.

Those who do it well have a culture of valuing people and are prepared to invest in it and it is driven through every level of the organization. Organizations that have succeeded appear to have had organizational values that support talent management and in many organizations it has occurred even without a formal strategy in place because of these organizational values. Without organizational values that support talent management, even a truly strategic and structured talent management approach will be difficult to achieve success with. It needs to be supported, committed to and lived out at all levels of the organization with strong and visible support and role models provided from the top.

2. **How do you spot talent in a new group of employees?**
    Their attributes, how they take to a new role, as well as the behaviours that they display, for example, using their initiative, drive and energy, commitment from an early stage and understanding the broader organization, not just their own role.

3. **You were brought up in Australia. Was there a different approach about your schooling, approach to work, talent?**
    I have been out of Australia for five years, so there may well have been new developments. However, there were similarities between the way Australia and the UK approach talent. In Australia there is a phrase that is commonly used to describe the country's cultural approach to success: 'cut down the tall poppies'. From a young age we were encouraged to be more humble, not to boast, not to talk too much or too openly about achievements. At school if you were 'gifted' the most support that you got was to take some classes with a higher grade. However, when as a child I went to the US for a year with my parents, who were teachers, the approach there was very different. I was assessed and then taken out of the normal class regularly for different classes on the gifted students programme. Many schools also had an Honour Roll, which acknowledged and celebrated those who achieved. It puts the criticism about the lack of humility in the US in context. In Australia, I worked for part of my career in recruitment and because we had a smaller market with fewer candidates to recruit for jobs, people were more open minded about attributes rather than technical skill. We would look at both EQ and IQ and the broader aspects of talent and would recruit across different industries and take those with the appropriate attributes and develop their technical skills on the job through training.

4. **What is the biggest challenge for talented people working in HR?**

    One of the major challenges for talented professionals working in HR is finding an organization that values best practice HR and allows HR to contribute to the strategic direction rather than just operate as a 'personnel function'. As HR has traditionally been perceived as a 'softer' function it can be more difficult in some organizations and circumstances for HR professionals to climb the business ladder to a GM or CEO position than other professionals coming through other routes such as finance or operations.

5. **Have you ever felt 'talent capped' in an organization? If so, what did you do about it?**

    Yes, I have at certain times, particularly in my early career. You often don't know how an organization truly views talent until you are in that organization. Many organizations don't have career paths. From very early in my career I was very driven and keen to develop and progress. At times in my career I found organizations didn't know how to support this. The way I coped was to find mentors who did value talent, to join professional organizations and business networks and think more broadly and creatively about how I could pursue my development goals. My ultimate ambition was, and is, less hierarchical and more to find the intellectual stimulus of the right role, to find alignment with my personal values and to make an impact in what can be perceived as a very intangible area.

6. **What are the significant actions that organizations can take to nurture talent?**

    It is key that talent management is never so broad and general that it loses sight of the individual and their value in the process. Talent management systems that are put in place for broad talent development, such as company-wide management fast track development programmes, need to be tailored. Talented individuals should be given priority access to development and provided with the encouragement and support to take up different job experiences within the organization. They should be given a greater chance for promotion and pushed (with support and development) with stretch activity and projects that will test their ability and resilience, creative thinking and commitment and give them an opportunity to develop and perform outside their skill and cultural comfort zones. Organizations should encourage talented people to network, to undertake peer and other coaching, to mentor and to be mentored. Horizontal progression and development should be encouraged as well as hierarchical progression.

7.   **How would you describe a talented person? Can you list some of the qualities, behaviours, competencies and the X factors that make a talented person different?**

High EQ, innovative, curious, empathetic, flexible and creative in their thinking, strength of character, prepared to stand up for what they believe in, ability to be collaborative and to work with diverse groups of people, passionate, entrepreneurial, empathetic and showing integrity.

8.   **What advice would you give talented people who feel that they have lost their way?**

If they are feeling disillusioned, or have reached a crossroads I would encourage them to step back and think about how they want to be stretched and then to present a clear business case for what development they are seeking. Talented people need to demonstrate how they can add value to an organization and take the initiative to present their value tangibly. It's also important to network both internally and externally and to learn from people. If they are feeling dissatisfied in their current role they should look at others who appear to be in a role or situation where they would like to be, take the opportunity to talk to them and to try to create a path to take them to that place. They may also need to take a reality check on whether the organization they are working with can offer/deliver what they need. It is important to look at yourself, your strengths and preferences and what you enjoy most and what you can bring to an organization as well as what the organization can bring to you.

9.   **Could you describe a perfect scenario when you really felt in tune with your talent, or in your ideal world how would you make best use of your talent?**

For me it is important to be recognized for my contribution. It's not just about money, although monetary reward can be important. Talented people are often driven to achieve, we want verbal recognition, to be valued for our commercial contribution. Being in learning and development, I feel self-aware and that I understand a lot about myself. I know what I enjoy and what I am passionate about. At times I had to take a leap of faith to pursue my interests and try something new. I have in the past made a backwards move in terms of pay; however, I knew that there was a potential new area of work where I could make a major contribution and that when I was passionate about something, and really interested in it, and enjoyed working hard at it, then the results and the rewards would follow.

Organizational support for work/life balance is also important. I am involved in a number of things outside the organization I work with. I learn German, I undertake Reiki, and I'm involved in a mentoring programme for underprivileged children through a programme called Roots and Wings.

10. Anything else you feel is important about talent?

If an organization raises expectations with talented employees then they must be prepared to meet them. It is one thing to identify talent, but organizations must know what to do with it once it has been identified! Progressive talent management needs to be about more than just succession planning, but also about supporting the individual in making a contribution and developing across the business.

It is important to look at your recruitment process and how you identify and attract talent. Organizations should ask 'Are we a magnet for talent?' Managers should be given the development that enables them to be great at identifying and recruiting talent. Creation of talent pools and networking with organizations such as universities and professional associations is key. Companies who truly understand talent management are always ready to hire talent irrespective of current needs.

Ultimately people are an organization's greatest resource. Organizations need to ask 'Does the amount of time, energy, money and focus we put into our talent equal the amount we put into hard capital?' If you recruit talented people into an organization it is important to recognize they may 'ruffle a few feathers' as they are curious, will challenge the status quo and stand up for what they believe.

There is not a shortage of talent, but instead a shortage of companies who are truly committed to providing talented people with the freedom to make their best contribution not constricted by bureaucracy and old-fashioned thinking and practices. Change management and communication is also key, as when people feel undervalued and unsettled it is the most talented employees who are likely to leave, as they are the ones who can find a job most easily.

It's a positive sign that more companies are working towards better talent management and we must ensure that true commitment, right from the top, is shown to really managing talent at all levels of organizations.

Contact details: caitycait6@yahoo.co.uk

TALENT – A PERSONAL VIEW: CLAYTON GLEN

Clayton Glen is currently Commercial Director with HDA (www.hda.co.uk), an international human capital consultancy based in London, specializing in organizational change facilitation, leadership development and career consultancy. Clayton has held senior HR roles (including HRD and International VP-HR) in the UK, the USA, continental Europe and in Southern Africa, in a range of industries, including chemicals/fmcg, automotive, e-commerce consulting and mobile technology. He has an MBA from the University of Wales.

1. **What is your opinion of how organizations in general treat talented people?**
    My experience is that organizations tend to use similar programme-based approaches to 'managing' high-potential people linked to company talent maps, succession plans, and so on, but often they are far off the mark, in that most of them are a little too static to address the developmental and career leverage needs of true talent. So, in effect, organizational talent tends to self-select outside of any formal talent management structure – some organizational talent stays and performs, and some leaves in spite of retention strategies and programmes that may be in place. The outcome is generally sub-optimal and few organizations manage it as well as they might if more responsive strategies were in place.

2. **How do you spot talent in a new group of employees?**
    It's context-specific. Organizations need blue-sky thinkers and leaders at some times, managers at others, and problem solvers at others... so spotting the right talent requires recognition that today's 'high potential' may in fact be either tomorrow's 'high flyer' or tomorrow's 'square peg in a round hole'. My experience is that organizations that set high stretch expectations up front, and create real opportunities for stretch (key projects, meaningful secondments, challenging assignments, etc) are best placed to spot real talent and to predict future success. Low-potential people generally self-select in any challenging context.

3. **You were brought up outside the UK. Was there a different approach about your schooling, approach to work, talent?**

    In South Africa the schooling system was rigorously academic with little streaming for different types of talent. You would either excel academically or not. If you did excel you would expect to go to university, but with little or no guidance on how to best apply your talent, or on how to consider your options for the future. University education was generally seen as an esoteric personal growth opportunity, with little vocational focus. That was my experience anyway. Those in the middle bracket academically would expect to attend a *technikon* (polytechnic), and this route was highly vocational, often with people going on to significant career successes. For those in the final bracket, embarking on a trade or joining a government department were pretty much the options. At the time in South Africa, one's race group was obviously also an issue in terms of final access to tertiary education in particular, so significant national talent – whole generations – will have been squandered. No doubt many highly talented people with significant potential were not given the opportunity to move beyond blue-collar roles.

4. **What is the biggest challenge for talented people working in HR?**

    Extricating themselves from primarily transactional activities, developing a strong commercial view, and becoming a competent and credible strategic influencer and trusted devil's advocate.

5. **Have you ever felt 'talent capped' in an organization? If so, what did you do about it?**

    Yes. The organization had a surfeit of recognized talent, including people who were considered amongst the best in the world in certain categories, eg we had one of the world's most recognized 'voice recognition' technologists, and a number of expert telecoms people who were considered leading edge in the industry. The environment was however by necessity project- and product-focused, as we were creating a new technology, and people largely focused on 'delivery' rather than on thinking strategically or beyond the 'brief' of what needed to be built to keep the investors happy. In reality, other than being associated with the building of a great new technology company, having a stake in the business, and having a surfeit of access to new learnings, the organization was not particularly competitive from a career development or rewards perspective. Equally, an extremely flat structure meant that there was little opportunity for upward progression.

I introduced a culture of 'career self-leverage' supported by a three-monthly career leverage review meeting for all team members across the company (UK, USA). The company culture encouraged 'self-stretch', and ensured that all team members were constantly reminded to make best use of their time at the organization, with the organization's view being that when we could no longer provide 'career stretch', talented people were likely to want to move on given opportunity cost considerations. The strategy was supported by a general culture of 'full disclosure and brutal honesty'. The outcome was zero turnover over a two year period, during a period of significant turnover and movement within the industry.

6.   **What are the significant actions that organizations can take to nurture talent?**
Manage it from the outset:

- introduce comprehensive 'buddying' for high-potential candidates before they join the organization, let them mentally become part of the team before they join it;
- develop a solid employer brand that flows through from recruitment, to selection, to hiring, to managing performance;
- ensure that talent stays engaged via mentoring, coaching and clear career expectation-setting;
- support it all with a simple, self-selecting and fast-moving talent management strategy.

7.   **How would you describe a talented person? Can you list some of the qualities, behaviours, competencies and the X factors that make a talented person different?**
Talented people have the right mix of emotional intelligence and energy. They know how to change their focus with changes in context – they are chameleons. Overall though, they create new ideas, solve problems and lead for organizational success.

8.   **What advice would you give talented people who feel that they have lost their way?**
Try out new things, create new opportunities and re-establish new paths to success. Working with a coach may be useful.

9.   **Could you describe a perfect scenario when you really felt in tune with your talent, or in your ideal world how would you make best use of your talent?**
Have never felt in tune. Ideal world – doing something that gives me pride, full engagement and ongoing challenge at the same time.

Contact details: cxg@hda.co.uk

TALENT – A PERSONAL VIEW: DENNIS PRESTON

Dennis Preston is an independent change management consultant and executive coach.

1. **What is your opinion of how organizations in general treat talented people?**

   I have a level of scepticism about HR using talent as another management fad, another way of jumping on the bandwagon of initiatives. Focusing on talent is only relevant if it matches business strategy, if, for example, where it is the organization's objective to develop talent to help them grow from where they are, to where they want to be. So if this process is devolved to HR it is critical that the HR director is genuinely plugged in to the business strategy – ideally at board level. It is also important to recognize that talented people are also the key to the future rather than the present.

2. **How do you spot talent in a new group of employees?**

   This can be quite a challenge: it is not the easiest thing to spot talent in a bunch of graduates, or new employees. Don't fall in to the trap of being easily impressed: it won't always be the loudest, or the person who speaks the longest, it is more likely to be the quiet one, who may sit at the back, who is more thoughtful. Often there is a slower process of talent emerging, where there is a payback over time.

3. **How did your schooling and initial approach to work impact on the development of your talent?**

   I don't know if I am talented. My formal education, my initial stabs at work, the start of learning new things, my academic background in a way had no real immediate relevance to my first work experiences. What work did give me was an opportunity to try different things, to find out what I enjoyed most over a long period of time. What traditional career management strategies do is allow people to progress in a prescribed way, but this is nothing to do with talent management, the development of quirky, lateral thinking people, who we identify to meet a need that we might not yet have. Unfortunately in a large organization, if the responsibility for developing this person is only given to HR it is unlikely that they will be able to achieve this in the broadest sense of talent development.

In a smaller organization you do get a better joined up picture and they may be able to carry on investing in someone who may not fit the organizational norm.

4. **What is the biggest challenge to talented people working in HR?**
    Staying in HR! It is an oxymoron! Get out as quick as possible; ask for secondment into a business area, a year in corporate finance, or operations. This doesn't just apply to HR, it also applies to people working in other vertical areas, eg IT: they should be encouraged to get out of their specialisms and to plug into different business areas.

5. **Have you ever felt 'talent capped' in an organization? If so, what have you done about it?**
    I was very fortunate in that I worked for two decent organizations who allowed me to move, to forge my own path of discovery, with organizational support. One of the most important tools for me is networking, talking to others, building trust and helping each other. Looking back this was a time when I was able to practise consultancy skills.

6. **What are the significant actions that organizations can take to nurture talent?**
    Organizations have a responsibility to support individuals, to give them space in their careers, to help them to make choices. There should be a structure that allows for access to excellent mentors (within the business) and excellent coaches (probably outside the organization). There should be opportunities to send individuals on secondments, overseas if possible. As well as planning for their departure, it is equally important to plan for their return. Another option can be sabbaticals, allowing individuals to have a year off, or to take a delayed gap year to go travelling, to discover what they really want out of work. Alternatively, encouraging flexible working can be very significant for talented people who have other interests and development areas outside of work.

7. **What advice would you give to talented people who have lost their way?**
    Explore with them the level of responsibility and risk that they are prepared to take. If they are within an organization getting them to explore what facilities exist that can help them to develop and grow. If they have exhausted those, to explore with them an exit plan. To take time out to explore what it might be like to work for themselves, to identify if they have either the drive, or the stamina to make it work.

8. **How would you describe a talented person, what are the qualities, behaviours, competencies and X factors that make a talented person?**

   People who contribute above and beyond what is expected, who challenge thinking at any level, who have a hunger, who question, who are impatient. They may be edgy, a loner, someone who doesn't fit into standard structures, can be seen as high-maintenance, they may also be seen as more of a taker than a giver.

9. **Can you describe a perfect scenario when you really felt in tune with your talent, or in an ideal world how would you make best use of your talent?**

   The best time for me was when I started to work for myself. A number of things that had not been clear before, clicked into place. It was a bit like when an amateur sports person makes up his or her mind to turn professional, there was that moment for me when I asked myself, 'Can I make a business and living for myself that I will really enjoy?' One massive driver for me is that I never stop learning.

10. **Any other comments?**

    There is a temptation when talking about talent to see it as an elite group; a special set of people. There is, however, something in everyone. It may not be the organization's responsibility to bring this out; not all talent is work-related.

    Great businesses have a clear business strategy of getting people ready to step into others' shoes; but it is a corporate responsibility to make the talent strategy work, not just HR's.

Contact details: anagram@dennispreston.co.uk

TALENT – A PERSONAL VIEW: DAVID PARKS

David Parks is vice president of Bluepoint Leadership Development.

1. **What is your opinion of how organizations in general treat talented people?**

   Talented people tend to be the busiest people in organizations because they get things done. The trouble is that due to their effectiveness, they become the 'go to' people to solve all manner of problems and projects. This in turn can lessen their effectiveness and dull their talent.

Smart organizations assign talented people to high-leverage challenges where there is going to be a bigger and better return on talent employed.

2. **How do you spot talent in a new group of employees?**
Whether in training or a real-life organizational setting, true talent will shine when presented with a *challenge*. Talented employees naturally rise up to a challenge and rally the necessary knowledge and resources to complete the challenge. You can usually spot them because they are ready and willing, attentive and eager, strategic and thoughtful.

3. **You were brought up in Northern Ireland. Was there a different approach about your schooling, approach to work, talent?**
I was brought up in Northern Ireland, have spent half my career in the UK and half in the US. My entire education was funded through government grants. In the US, education comes at a cost, a very high cost, and almost all students have to work whilst studying to pay their way and pay off student loans for years afterwards. I know things have changed in the UK but the fees are still nowhere near university fees in the US.

I left the UK in 1996. A personal driver for this move was really to stretch myself and turn work into much more of an adventure. The highly entrepreneurial culture in the US is much more conducive to risk-taking and breeds a 'can do' attitude. My schooling and the values instilled by my parents was never about money, it was about a good education and career. Money tends to be a bigger part of the equation in the US and is definitely a bigger driver than in the UK.

4. **What is the biggest challenge for talented people working in HR?**
The biggest challenge might be to overcome the traditional stereotypes that are attached to the HR function. My advice for talented people in HR is to be business people first and HR people second. Get squarely behind the business goals, to the point of running your HR department like an outsourced professional service firm. I would encourage all HR professionals to ask themselves 'Would the service I provide sell on the open market?'

5. **Have you ever felt 'talent capped' in an organization? If so, what did you do about it?**
Yes. I worked in a very rigid culture at one company in the UK. My managing director was a former military man and ran the company like a military battalion. My approach was to chip away incessantly

at the corporate culture to loosen it up. I constantly tested the limits in a very calculated way and chose my battles very carefully.

I put a lot of passion and energy into the job, but towards the end of my tenure I was definitely looking for an exit strategy. I did not feel my talents were being fully utilized or appreciated. Ironically, it is only after resigning a job that most talented people are told the value that they have contributed.

6. **What are the significant actions that organizations can take to nurture talent?**

As a practitioner of leadership development, I strongly believe that the number one job of a leader is to nurture and grow the next generation of talent. Creating a culture of development is a key component. Formal training such as high-potential leadership programs, stretch assignments, on-the-job projects, coaching and mentoring are all vital ingredients.

The most influential factor by far to nurture talent is the relationship that the talent has with their manager. Great managers naturally view themselves as coaches who want to see their talented direct reports blossom and grow. Managers need to constantly ask themselves: How am I showing up as a leader? Am I providing clear direction and the right challenges? Am I enabling (or disabling) my people? Am I open to new ideas? Do I care about this person's development?

7. **How would you describe a talented person? Can you list some of the qualities, behaviours, competencies and the X factors that make a talented person different?**

I think a key factor is to do with the paradox of the 'head' and the 'heart'. Talented people both display the logical left side of the brain and show a high emotional quotient. Aside from this talented people are generally innovative, positive, creative and tenacious around goals. Talented people are the ones who generally get things done to a very high standard and with panache and creative flair.

8. **What advice would you give talented people who feel that they have lost their way?**

Take stock of who you are, what you stand for, what you love, what you hate, where you want to go in life. Basically do a life audit thinking back to times in your career and life where you have felt most alive, energized and productive. Looking back will provide some good answers, but you have got to look forward too.

When I interview talent, I often ask 'How would you like to write the next chapter of your life?' or 'In twenty years' time, when you look back, what will be the things that you wish you did?'

9. **Could you describe a perfect scenario when you really felt in tune with your talent, or in your ideal world how would you make best use of your talent?**

My present role involves organizing and deploying leadership development consultants to deliver programs mostly with Fortune 1,000 companies. My ideal vision is that the work that we do is good enough to be written up in the Harvard Business Review. That is my vision and my benchmark, which naturally sets a high level of expectation and a compelling vision.

I work with a team of very talented consultants. The best thing that I can do for them is to set them up for success with as comprehensive briefing as possible on the client goals and business challenges. In turn, they keep me posted on progress, problems and opportunities and ensure that we are all working for the greater good of the client.

10. **Anything else you feel is important about talent?**

I think one of the keys to successful talent management is to treat each individual as an individual. Great leaders truly care and appreciate the talent that works for them, they confront and challenge them in a unique way and they will hold their talent accountable for results.

David Parks is VP of Sales and Marketing. Part of the senior team founding Bluepoint Leadership Development, David originally joined the Tom Peters Company in 1996. He is responsible for leading sales development activity at Bluepoint. This includes the acquisition and development of major clients such as Microsoft, Nike, Seagate Technology, Cisco Systems and GE. He describes his role as 'oiling the wheels of business and helping organizations realize their strategic goals'. When not transforming the world of work, David is a keen athlete, a former rugby player turned triathlete who has swum the Golden Gate and 'Escaped from Alcatraz' many times. He, his wife Shirley, daughter Fiona and son Conor live in the San Francisco Bay Area.

Contact details: davidparks@bluepointleadership.com

12

The basis of our research

The foundations of our research started in education. One of the authors (Kaye Thorne) originally trained as a teacher and as part of her studies became interested in the work of E. Paul Torrance and his studies of creativity and children. In addition to developing the most widely used tests of creativity, Torrance also created the 'Future Problem Solving Program', and developed the 'Incubation Model of Teaching'. He authored dozens of books and more than 2,000 published articles on creativity during the course of his career. Torrance's 2001 book, *Manifesto: A Guide to Developing a Creative Career,* includes the results of his 40-year longitudinal study of creativity – the only one of its kind.

This interest in creativity continued into her consulting and coaching work with adults. As part of her research for her book *Managing the Mavericks* (2003) Kaye spent time interviewing and conducting a survey with individuals who identified themselves as being creative or innovative, or who could be described as 'maverick'. The questionnaire invited them to identify the issues, the opportunities and the culture that helped them to develop their individual creativity and enabled organizations to innovate.

'What became very special for me', says Kaye, 'was that as the e-mails came through, the willingness of people to take part, the thoughtfulness of their responses, the commitment to send the questionnaire on to others in their network, not just as a questionnaire but often with a personal endorsement, and a genuine interest and encouragement in the whole process happened on a global basis.' The results of the responses to the questionnaires were non-attributed, which gave people a freedom to be more honest in their responses. In addition, another group of people agreed to be interviewed as case studies.

The responses of both groups gave a privileged insight; their candour, comments, challenges and questions have given a richness of observation, which uniquely takes us close to their day to day reality of trying to do things differently. There is valuable advice for organizations, some very poignant statements about some of the challenges faced by individuals in making personal choices about whether to stay or leave an organization; or to have the courage to believe in themselves enough to do what they really wanted to do. This was balanced against the independence and freedom felt by those who were working for themselves.

These are people with a very different outlook on life. Call them mavericks, call them innovative, there is not really an appropriate label that sums them up. My belief is that every individual is unique, but added to this uniqueness there are some people who are living with something else that presents them and the people or organizations with whom they interact, the opportunity to really make a difference in this world of ours. Their responses provide some fresh insights, wisdom and another level of input into the ongoing challenge of raising the awareness and recognition of the importance of creativity and innovation as one of the key foundation stones of organizational development. As well as providing background information for the book, we have also referred to some of the findings in this book. It also resulted in a paper called 'Mavericks Talking' (available from contact@theinspirationnetwork.co.uk). The questionnaire is reproduced below.

Managing the Mavericks **questionnaire**

All responses will be non-attributable and used only to develop quantifiable and qualitative research data, the results of which will be circulated to all respondents and used in *Managing the Mavericks* book.

1. Thinking back over your learning experiences, how do you prefer to learn?

2. What are the best conditions that help you to be creative/innovative?

3. In an ideal world how do you like to work?

   – environment?

- hours?
- work colleagues?
- management style?
- employed?
- self-employed?

4. How much responsibility do you want?
    - managing yourself?
    - managing others?
    - managing process?

5. What are your sources of inspiration?

6. What is the hardest part of being creative?

7. What is the most rewarding part of being creative?

8. What does your organization do that inhibits creativity and innovation?

9. What does your organization do to stimulate creativity and innovation?

10. How would you define a maverick?

11. What do you think mavericks want from an organization?

12. If you could change one aspect of organizations that would encourage the nurturing of talent, what would you recommend?

Is there anything else that you would like to add?
Thank you for completing this questionnaire.

As part of our research for this book we also circulated to a different group of people the questionnaire below, the findings of which are included in this book. Again the responses were non-attributed, but in addition we also interviewed some other people who were prepared to share their views on talent. These are reproduced in Chapter 11: Talent – a personal view.

Talent questionnaire (individual)

All responses will be non-attributable and used only to develop quantifiable and qualitative research data, the results of which will be circulated to all respondents and used in the forthcoming _Talent Management_ book.

1. How old were you when you first realized that you might be talented? Was it because of someone else's suggestion?

2. What were your experiences like at school? Was your talent supported?

3. What is the hardest part of being talented?

4. What do you enjoy most about being talented?

5. Have you ever felt 'talent capped' within an organization? What did you do as a result?

6. Do you ever feel that you have more talent than your organization needs? How do you channel your excess talent in, or out of work?

7. What do you do to develop your own talent?

8. How do you want to be managed?

9. What are the significant actions that organizations can take to nurture talent?

10. How would you describe a talented person? Can you list some of the qualities, behaviours, competencies, or the X factors that makes a talented person different?

11. Can you describe a perfect scenario when you really felt in tune with your talent, or in your ideal world how would you make best use of your talent?

12. Any other comments?

Thank you for completing this questionnaire, the findings will be circulated later this year.

We also used the following questionnaire as the basis for our case studies in this book.

Talent management questionnaire (organization)

All responses will be non-attributable and used only to develop quantifiable and qualitative research data, the results of which will be circulated to all respondents and used in the forthcoming *Talent Management* book.

1. What does your organization do to create a culture and climate to encourage the learning potential of all employees?

2. How do you attract, engage and retain talented people?

3. Who drives the process and which departments were involved?

4. How have you managed the ongoing expectations of talented people?

5. What are the biggest challenges in managing talent within your organization?

6. How have these been overcome?

7. What have been the benefits (particularly business ones)?

8. What measures or processes have you put in place to measure the effectiveness of your talent strategy?

9. What advice would you give to others?

Thank you for completing this questionnaire; the findings will be circulated later this year.

In addition to this Kaye had also undertaken some research into the management of talent for a guide called 'One Stop Guide to Talent Management' for _Personnel Today_, which she co-authored (2003).

Both Andy and Kaye have undertaken a number of talent consulting and coaching assignments with clients, which have added to our ongoing source of knowledge. It is a topic that is very close to our hearts.

Note: Copies of _Managing the Mavericks_ originally published by Spiro Publishing are now available from kaye@theinspirationnetwork.co.uk.

References

Bennis, W and Biederman, P W (1997) *Organizing Genius: The Secrets of Creative Collabration*, Nicholas Brealey, London

Breen, Bill (2001) 'Where are you on the talent map?' *Fast Company*, December

Brown, Phillip and Hesketh, Anthony (2004) *The Mismanagement of Talent*, Oxford University Press, Oxford

Buckingham, M (2005) *The One Thing You Need to Know*, Simon & Schuster, London

Cameron, J (2002) *Walking in this World*, Rider, London

Cook, Peter (2006) *Sex, Leadership and Rock 'n' Roll*, Crown House Publishing, London

Csikszentmihalyi, Mihaly (1990) *Flow*, Harper & Row, London

Davenport, Thomas H (2005) *Thinking For a Living: How to Get Better Performance and Results From Knowledge Workers*, Harvard Business School Press, Boston

Dyson, J (1998) *Against the Odds: An Autobiography*, Trafalgar Square, London

Edvinsson, L and Malone, Michael S (1997) *Intellectual Capital*, Piatkus, London

Eikleberry, Carol (1995) *The Career Guide for Creative and Unconventional People*, Ten Speed Press, Berkeley, California

Gardner, Howard (1983) *Frames of Mind*, BasicBooks, NY

Gardner, Howard (1997) *Extraordinary Minds*, Phoenix (Orion), London

Gelb, Michael (1998) *How to Think Like Leonardo da Vinci*, Thorsons, London

Gilbert, I (2002) _Essential Motivation in the Classroom_, Routledge, Falmer

Goleman, Daniel (1998) _Working with Emotional Intelligence_, Bantam, New York

Goleman, Daniel, Boyatzis, Richard and McKee, Annie (2002) _The New Leaders_, Little, Brown, London

Hammonds, Keith H (2005) 'Why We Hate HR' _Fast Company_, August

Handy, Charles (1995) _Beyond Certainty_, Hutchinson, London

Intellectual Property (2001) CBI and KPMG, Caspian Publishing, London

Kao, John (1996) _Jamming: The Art and Discipline of Business Creativity_, HarperCollins, London

Koib, D A, Rubin, I M and McIntyre, J M (1994) Organisational Psychology: An experiential approach to organisational behaviour, 4th edn, Prentice Hall, London

Manville, Brook and Foote, Nathaniel (1996) 'Strategy as if knowledge mattered' in _Fast Company_, April

Michaels, E, Handfield-Jones, H and Axelrod, B (2001) _The War for Talent_, Harvard Business School Press, Boston

Muoio, Anna (2000) 'Man with a (talent) plan' in _Fast Company_, December

O'Reilly, C A and Pfeffer, J (2000) _Hidden Value: How Great Companies Achieve Extraordinary Results with Ordinary People_, Harvard University Press, Boston

Peters, Tom (1997) _The Circle of Innovation_, Hodder & Stoughton, London

Pritchett, P and Pound, R (1994) _High Velocity Culture Change_, Pritchett & Associates, Dallas

Salovey, P, Mayer, J D and Caruso, D R (1997) 'Emotional Intelligence Meets Traditional Standards for an Intelligence', unpublished document

Seldes, George (1978) _Great Quotations_, Pocket, New York

Semler,Ricardo (1993) _Maverick_, Arrow, London

Senge, Peter M (1990) _The Fifth Discipline_, Doubleday, New York

Senge, P, Scharmer, O, Jaworski, J and Flowers, B (2004) _Presence_, Nicholas Brealey, London

Thorne, Kaye (2003) _Managing the Mavericks_, Spiro Publishing, London

Thorne, Kaye (2004) _Coaching for Change_, Kogan Page, London

Torrance, E Paul (2002) _Manifesto: A Guide to Developing a Creative Career_, Ablex Publishing, Westport, Conn

Ulrich, D and Brockbank, W (2005) _The HR Value Proposition_, Harvard Business School Press, Boston

Woodhouse, Mark and Thorne, Kaye (2003) 'One Stop Guide to Talent Management' _Personnel Today Management Resources_, Reed Publishing, Surrey

Recommended reading

Butler, P et al (1997) 'A revolution in interaction' *McKinsey Quarterly*, No 1: 8.

Buzan, Tony (2001) *Head Strong*, Thorsons, London

Fowler, H W and Fowler, F G (1995) *Concise Oxford Dictionary*, 9th edn, Oxford University Press, Oxford

McNally, David (1993) *Even Eagles Need a Push*, Thorsons, London

Morton, V (ed.) (1999) *Corporate Fundraising*, Charities Aid Foundation, Kent, Institute of Charity Fundraising Managers, London

Ridderstråle, J and Nordstrom, K, (2000) *Funky Business*, ft.com, London

Semler, Ricardo (2003) *The Seven-Day Weekend*, Random House, London

Slater, Robert (1998) *Jack Welch and the GE Way — Management Insights and Leadership Secrets Of the Legendary CEO*, McGraw Hill, New York

Thorne, Kaye (2001) *Personal Coaching: releasing potential at work*, Kogan Page, London

Thorne, Kaye (2004) 'Employer Branding' *Personnel Today Management Resources*, Reed Publishing, Surrey

Thorne, Kaye and Machray, Alex (1999) *World Class Training* Kogan Page, London

US Bureau of Labour Statistics (1999) 'Labour Force 2008' in *Monthly Labour Review*, November

Index

Other books by the same author

Blended Learning: How to integrate online and traditional learning, Kaye Thorne, 2002, Kogan Page

Coaching for Change: Practical strategies for transforming performance, Kaye Thorne, 2004, Kogan Page

Everything You Ever Needed to Know About Training, Kaye Thorne and David Mackey, 2003, Kogan Page

Personal Coaching: Releasing potential at work, Kaye Thorne, 2001, Kogan Page

World Class Training, Alex Machray and Kaye Thorne, 1999, Kogan Page

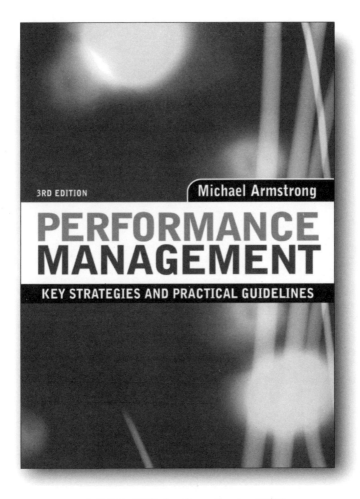